MW01618118

Sorry
~~Carloyn~~ Carolyn

PRESENTED TO

Thank You!
Enjoy--

Lonnetta Kelly

FROM

6-14-2023

DATE

Proverbs 3: 5-6

PRAISE FOR JOY IN THE HEARTLAND

While reading Lonnette Kelley's book *Joy in the Heartland,* I spent an afternoon lost in the amazing pictures and the stories of her travels in her home state of South Dakota. While I had been to the state many times, much of what I was reading about and seeing was new to me.

I was put in the mood for this relaxing book by the introduction story about her father taking the family on vacation without planning the trip. Vacations with my family were much the same when I was growing up. My dad was too busy making a living to plan those types of things.

The stories about the travels were interesting, and the pictures made the ordinary seem breathtaking as my imagination ran wild through the history of these places and basically, just the small-town feel, much like where I grew up in Tennessee. As she says in the *Ageless Prairie Trail* chapter, "Memories are the bridge between the past, present, and the future!"

The sadness of Covid-19 was always in the backdrop, and the story of attending funerals online was all too familiar. Yet the truth in that made the stories even more real.

Some of the highlights to me were the *Farmland Trail* chapter or, as I call it, the '*Red*' chapter, and especially the Texaco station, that was a flash from the past. I was moved by the pictures of 'The Way and 'Victory over Death in the *Lake Country Trail* chapter.

All in all, I would recommend this book and taking the time to enjoy these trails. Sometimes we all need to take a breath and just get out and enjoy this beautiful country and realize that as Americans, God has blessed us with a great place to explore.

— **MARK HOUSER**
Singer-songwriter
Find out more at Americanaville.net and markhouserbluegrass.com

Author Lonnette Kelley takes readers along an interactive journey through southeastern South Dakota and the small towns within that region in a unique and special way. Her book showcases rural South Dakota and small-town America at its finest. With each section and each photograph, you will be whisked away into exploring each of these special communities. Readers will be encouraged to embark on their own adventure down the ten different trails you may take to find "The Heart" of each community. It is then, once out on your own expedition, that you will truly understand the exhilaration and joy that the author felt.

— **JARED HYBERTSON,**
Community & Economic Development Coordinator-City of Centerville, SD -Executive Director-Centerville Development Corporation, President-Centerville Chamber of Commerce-County Commissioner-Turner County, SD

Lonnette Kelley is the friend, mom, and grandma everyone never knew they always needed. Creative, fun-loving, and visionary, she has a passion to help people love their homeland the way she does. This book offers experiences of quality family time, pioneering, and discovery. Own this special personal tour guide, and you'll have opportunities for staycations all year long. Don't forget to pack a picnic!

— **CHRISTINE TRACY**
Author of *Tapestry, The Divine Design for Your Life*

Lonnette is passionate about making life an adventure, regardless of what is going on in her life or in the world. It's easy to feel as if you're on an adventure with her. Lonnette's enthusiasm and creativity spark a great desire to go on the adventures she narrates in her new book.

— **LISA FAHEY,**
Author, Speaker, and Coach

Lonnette Kelley is one amongst us who has an idea and goes with it. What a great idea she had for this book and getting neighboring South Dakota communities to know each other better.

— **CLEO, IRENE, South Dakota**

It has been an honor to watch Lonnette share her journey of writing "Joy in the Heartland" during such a critical time in our history. I highly recommend her book as she expresses so beautifully from her own heart, through eyes of faith, her love for America, and the many wonderful people she met along the way.

I believe you will be encouraged, experience joy, and find new hope as you hear her account of what she discovered along the way.

— **PJ CLARK,**
Artist, Author, and Speaker www.DesertThunderArts.com

I've known Lonnette for a few years now. What has always stood out to me is her love for Jesus and her spreading joy and love to others. Her book, "Joy in the Heartland," was born out of looking for a way to find enjoyment during a time when many were fearful and struggling with isolation. Lonnette is not one to settle for sitting around, so she and her friend set out on a journey to find meaning and purpose in this trying time. What she found was joy and, in her usual fashion, sought a way to share what she discovered. "Joy in the Heartland" is her invitation to us to join her in the journey and experience our own joy along the way.

— **JUDEE,** Sioux Falls, South Dakota

Lonnette Kelley is a trusted friend I rely on because she always does as she says she will. She has been faithful as we work together with The Christian Women's Connections, bringing hope into the lives of other women. She is encouraging with her positive and uplifting support.

Her life is an example of how God can take a broken heart and insert joy.

Lonnette is fun-loving and values adventure. She loves Jesus and her book shows ways God gives purpose and light to a hurting world. I highly recommend this book as an energizing guide to discovering little-known information about southeastern South Dakota, bringing it like a lighthouse to a dark world. Lonnette's story also demonstrates the redemptive power of faith and the ability to seek joy in all circumstances.

— **KRIS, BRANDON,** South Dakota

Lonnette Kelley is a woman of faith. Whenever facing the darkest times in her life, she has taken all things to the Lord and counted on Him to help her through.

We are friends, but meeting her and becoming friends was not by chance. It was a "Godwink" or Divine Intervention for me. God has people and events standing all along our journey, ready to help us reach that Divine intervention. It is up to each of us to listen to God and allow Him to help us. I believe that God was totally in control of our friendship. As a result, we are both blessed.

Lonnette inspires me by her striving to become a better Christian, serving others on a daily basis. She shares a light for all and gives joy to those around her. She has a strong character and lives by offering others her thoughtful ways and encouraging their faith to grow through her wisdom and the impact of her personal prayer.

— **LINDA C.,** Sioux Falls, South Dakota

Lonnette Kelley is a friend. As nurses, we served on the local Quick Response team and many other services, sharing our lives, family and friends throughout many moments over the years. Lonnette is a woman of integrity; she loves Jesus with all her heart and lives out daily what she believes. "Joy in the Heartland" is Lonnette's true story of her search during difficult times to discover joy. This journey ultimately brings an exciting hunt to southeastern South Dakota so that others may also discover joy.

— **SHERRY,** Mountain, North Dakota

Lonnette Kelley is a woman of compassion, which is shown in everything she does. She is an authentic genuine healer of hearts. Her desire is to give hope to all that they will know their purpose in this life. For example, she is a way-shower of how very simple it is to share joy with others in a fun-loving way.

— **NANCY M.,**
Clinical Hypnotherapist CHT, CMS, NLP

Lonnette Kelley has a caring personality, positive nature and strong faith. She is very creative and "Joy in the Heartland" will continue Lonnette's mission to touch many lives bringing them joy.

— **EARL M.**

JOY IN THE *Heartland*

ISBN Softcover: 978-1-7379743-0-7

Printed in the United States of America.

Cover and Interior Design: Heidi Caperton
Cover Image: Kathy Zimmel and Peggy Hentges
Editor: Kendra Paulton
Proofing Editor: Vicki Prentice
Photographer: Lonnette Kelley

www.joyintheheartland.com

JOY IN THE Heartland

Life-Changing Road Trips Through
God's Living Fields of South Dakota

LONNETTE KELLEY

DEDICATION

To my son Michael, a precious gift from God. 1977-2018

For all who seek a better day, may this journey lead you to joy and everlasting life.

It is not until we look back into our past that we truly appreciate all the dreams, visions and love each generation carried forward just for us! To all who have walked before me, I say thank you from the bottom of my heart!

When everything is gone and fear fills the empty chair, remember there is power in a smile!

THANK YOU TO MY SPONSORS

Jeremy Brown, Throne Publishing

Crystal Carlson, Liberty Tax Service

Allan C. Fisher, visual artist/owner

TABLE OF CONTENTS

Foreword . . . . *xix*

Introduction . . . . *xxi*

Preface . . . . *xxv*

Join the Photo Hunt . . . . *xxix*

State Parks & Recreation Information . . . . *xxxi*

Chapter 1: Sioux Valley Trail 33

Chapter 2: Heartland Trail 51

Chapter 3: Wetland Trail 69

Chapter 4: Big Sioux River Trail 85

Chapter 5: Old West Trail 103

Chapter 6: Farmland Trail 117

Chapter 7: Ageless Prairie Trail 133

Chapter 8: Harvest Trail 153

Chapter 9: Lake Country Trail 173

Chapter 10: Siouxland Trail 195

Conclusion: Sunset Trail 216

Note of Appreciation *223*

Acknowledgments *227*

About the Author *229*

FOREWORD

I was sorting through my emails like any other day when I ran across one from a woman seeking a proofreader for her soon-to-be-published book, Joy in the Heartland. The idea of proofreading Lonnette Kelley's book intrigued me, yet my initial reaction was that I didn't have time to take on the project. As I progressed through my emails, I couldn't shake the feeling that deep down, this sounded like something I really wanted to do. When I talked to my husband, he agreed that this was an opportunity I should not pass up.

So I dialed her up, and am I ever glad I did! The more Lonnette explained her book and how she came to write it, the more excited I got! It quickly became apparent to both of us that God had brought the two of us together.

Joy in the Heartland is set in the year 2020, when Lonnette Kelley, like most of us, found herself bored, lonely, and searching for purpose as she sheltered in place during the Covid-19 pandemic. Determined not to let it get her down, she armed herself with a bit of creativity, a spirit of adventure, and a desire to find some joy. She grabbed her camera and a friend with a pickup truck, and they took their first of many drives within a fifty-mile radius of her Sioux Falls, South Dakota, home.

Lonnette's stories and original photographs will inspire you to explore the same 51 communities Lonnette and her driver did, whether or not you live near Sioux Falls. Even if you don't live in the area or have plans to visit anytime soon, her stories will challenge you to discover the wealth of blessings and joy right in your own backyard.

You don't want to miss Lonnette's invitation to step away from the darkness, the chaos, and stresses of daily life to find peace and joy. Follow Lonnette on her joy journey through the ten trails of southeastern South Dakota, and you will make memories and experience the God of creation. But don't just read the book–which is truly an adventure in itself–but make plans to live the adventure, for that is where you will find the real joy.

Today, as I write this, I have not yet had the privilege of meeting Lonnette in person, yet I feel as though I have known her for years. I found every one of our phone conversations uplifting and encouraging, as it was with every page of her book.

Lonnette possesses a strong faith in God that she is not afraid to share. Her personable grace draws you into her story in a way that encourages and uplifts. Her fun-loving personality juxtaposed with her serious "Driver" depicted in their travels often made me smile–even laugh–as I was reminded how good it is to appreciate those who differ from us on this incredible journey we call life.

Vicki L. Prentice
This Life Legacy
Wessington, South Dakota

INTRODUCTION

I remember the days when my family would pack and pack until everyone was completely worn out, and then we would collapse into our car just to drive all through the night. Even though we needed rest, the word "vacation" was to take care of that.

Not being very good at making plans, my dad often found himself in difficult situations. During these brief vacations, we searched madly for this thing called rest. With just a few hours in each day, there simply was not enough time for my dad to plan and organize a so-called perfect vacation. His idea was to drive all day, wander impulsively from place to place checking out whatever sights we happened to stumble across, until suddenly realizing it was time to find a bed.

For the next hour or two, we madly chased down neon signs, looking for the one, and only one, that offered a vacancy. One night in particular I remember my mom, dad, and us two little girls sitting on a hard wooden bench until the wee hours of the morning staring down the desk clerk until she finally gave in and returned our room charge. It seems my sister had spotted a cockroach.

Seventy-plus years later, I again found myself hostage to a bug. This new bug was called a virus—Covid-19 to be exact—and it was creating a pandemic throughout the world, the likes of which had never been seen. For some unexplainable reason, the focus of the virus appeared to be the elderly and others with health conditions. I

was now a prime target, along with most of my friends. Death was all around us, and the world went into isolation.

In this land of sorrow with no place to go and every event canceled, it was difficult to awaken day after day to the same old, same old. Some type of purpose was needed and my creativity began to take hold. I knew I had been blessed; I was not in this pandemic alone like so many others. I had a friend to share my quirky ideas with and we had a common bond: we enjoyed long peaceful drives in the country, and I liked snapping pictures.

It didn't take long before this pair of senior citizens was cruising the back roads of southeastern South Dakota. With no plans, (I wonder where this lack of planning came from) we were out of the house. Freedom was ours for a few hours and that's all that mattered. Our focus became unique camera shots that would someday land us a prized photo—the more out of the ordinary, the better.

In a world struggling with darkness and despair, we found ourselves being filled with happiness and joy that could not be explained, and began thinking of how this same experience could be shared. Determined to share our adventure, we set a fifty-mile radius around the city of Sioux Falls, and divided the region into ten small-town communities, creating what I now call "The Ten Trails of the Heartland."

To our surprise, we discovered complimenting parks, glacial lakes, winding rivers, and valleys, that added an extra touch of fun and relaxation to each trail. We agreed some of our more enjoyable moments throughout this experience came with our search for unusual and interesting photos. It was decided we would create the same type of hunt, only reverse the idea and display our photos for others to seek as they explored each trail.

The goal of our adventure is to bring everyone into the Heartland. We felt it only right to help others know more about whom they are visiting. Your search for the heart and tidbits of information will help introduce you to the 51 neighboring towns in this journey while creating a hunger to learn more and understand the blessings and beauty of this wonderful region.

Joy in the Heartland is a story filled with laughter and tears as you follow this pair of trailblazers through their wild and complicated journey during the 2020 pandemic. If you are looking for an inspiring adventure, this is it! These two explorers were about to make the discovery that somewhere in all the uncertainty and sadness there was a plan tucked away...just waiting for them.

PREFACE

I am sitting at my kitchen table. I have things that need to be done today but my mind is taking me back to the farm, which is always a great escape when I need to hide for a while. But today, I am being led to another moment when things weren't as glorious as I had hoped.

I heard screams coming across the farmyard and immediately jumped into action to see what was happening. One of my dad's newly hired helpers was trying to ride a bale of hay up the elevator into the barn when his leg became caught in the elevator. With each scream, his leg was twisted tighter and tighter toward a horrific end. My dad and I reached the power pole at the same time, and amazingly, after some serious work to unwind this young man's leg, he walked away with just a few bruises. Oh, the joy of that moment!

What if you had the chance to live a new life, to step away from the darkness, the chaos, and stresses of daily living, no matter the bruises, and walk again in peace and joy? What if you had the chance each day to deliberately seek joy, slow your pace, find restful meadows, and take a deeper look into the hearts of those around you? Well, you do—that's what my book is about. Today can be your new beginning!

Last year, when the pandemic struck, my 55-year career in nursing came to a sudden stop. With pain and sadness everywhere, having been on the front lines of nursing all my life, I was suddenly without purpose. Finding myself isolated, I cried out, "Lord, what can I do to help?" After discovering a new set of paints, I decided to calm my thoughts and try my hand at some type of artistic design. To this point, painting walls had been my expertise. I was now facing a challenging new adventure with a piece of paper and a small brush in front of me.

Soon I found myself surrounded by cute wide-eyed animals seeming to be speaking directly to my heart. One animal shouted, "Do not fear, I am with you." Another animal quietly whispered, "Things are going to be all right. We are God's messengers. We will carry a smile, words of encouragement, and hope to all. Your part, Lonnette, is to stay safe and keep us marching." Today, these little animals continue to carry God's Spirit of hope and love throughout the country. It has been a busy year; together, we have placed over 4,000 cards of hope in the hands of the lonely, those gripped in pain and fear, and others whose future is unclear.

The Lord knew my dedication, but apparently, he also knew I needed to be refreshed. It wasn't long before a photo contest caught my eye, and a friend asked if I wanted to go for a ride. I grabbed my camera, and soon little drives in the country replaced the darkness of each day. Searching for joy, we experienced six months of excitement and fun challenges throughout southeastern South Dakota, while gathering memories for a lifetime. With our eyes opened wide, we found all things new. Our hearts filled with love for each community and for our forefathers who gave their all so that we could enjoy the blessings of this beautiful country!

Today, this same experience can be yours. Come join the fun. Joy is everywhere–all you need is the desire to find it. *Joy in the Heartland* will be your guide as you travel the ten trails of southeastern South Dakota. Adding challenge to your journey, fifty-one hearts, photos, and unending treasures are hidden–one in each town–for all to discover. Embrace each moment, rediscover laughter, wonder, intrigue, mystery, gratitude, history, friendship, and love! *Joy in the Heartland* will encourage families and bring generations together to make memories, share stories, and create an unforgettable experience rooted in South Dakota and God Himself. Do not miss out. Pack some hotdogs, roasting sticks, and a few sodas. Your adventure is waiting!

Oath of a trailblazer

I will be determined to discover something new. I will find joy in the moments and appreciate the journey. I will communicate where I am and where I am headed for the safety of all. I will follow directions and heed all warnings. I will respect and protect the beauty and goodness of each trail for the enjoyment of others to follow. I will share this journey in word or photo with those less fortunate that they may also find joy and happiness.

Thank you for reading this Preface. May the road ahead lead you to everlasting joy!

JOIN THE PHOTO HUNT

First: Stay safe!

The idea of this hunt is to simply enjoy the journey!

Joy in the Heartland is your go-to book for the locations of trails, lists of photos, community information, and recreation areas of this epic adventure. Each individual or team choosing to join this exciting hunt will select one of the Ten Trails of the Heartland, take a good look at the photos listed for that trail, and begin the search. The goal is to explore and gain a better understanding of each community as you seek and find the red hand-painted wooden hearts and one or more photos from each of the 51 towns I've written about.

These 10" x 10" hearts won't be too hard to spot. You're likely to find them attached to a building, a tree, something of great value or historical interest, or anywhere else that might be considered the heart of the community.

You can see each heart and all 300 photo sites from your car as you drive calmly through city streets, so there is no need for trespassing on private property. Of the 300 photos, 159 of them are unique photos I captured in the 51 communities. Also, for your enjoyment, I have included an additional 141 original photos depicting the beautiful scenery and peaceful moments we saw along the way.

Wear your seatbelt and respect all speed limits. When interacting within each community, be sure you are always polite and respectful. You do not want complaints to ruin the hunt for others or create problems for the future.

I took all the photos featured in this book in 2020, doing my best to select various shots that would have longevity. However, in a world that seems to be in a state of constant change, some treasures may disappear over time. In that case, you are welcome to be creative and search for your own unique photo opportunities.

Should you wish to share your adventure, please keep us updated by emailing your stories and photos to www.joyintheheartland.com. We will keep track on our website and share your stories. By sending your photos, you agree to allow us to use your photo on social media and other outlets as a promotional tool for *Joy in the Heartland*.

Spoiler Alert
Please keep each heart and photo location secret that others may also enjoy the journey.

Don't forget to search for the big red heart hidden in plain sight in each of the following towns!

STATE PARKS & RECREATION INFORMATION

South Dakota Game, Fish and Parks
523 East Capitol Ave
Pierre, SD 57501

Hunting and Fishing:
WildInfo@state.sd.us

Parks and Recreation:
ParkInfo@state.sd.us

Customer Service:
605-223-7660

#SDInTheField

Sioux Valley Trail

CHAPTER 1

SIOUX VALLEY TRAIL

"Hidden among the hustle and bustle in the backyards of our lives, joy quietly calls out our names, waiting patiently for us to seek it."

Under the warm summer sun, everything appeared like a fresh new painting. The croplands, farms, and everything surrounding seemed so bright, colorful, and full of life. It kept my camera busy. Like a well-planned oasis, every few miles a beautiful church with its cross held high would rise above the trees and welcome two old friends into its little town. For the moment darkness had been dulled and freedom was ours.

When morning reflected the beginnings of a beautiful day, the obituary section in our daily newspaper argued otherwise. Death was in the air circling like a vulture looking for prey and we were wearing its choice colors: old age and other health concerns.

In March 2020, due to no fault of our own, the life we had known for seventy-plus years instantly stopped. We found ourselves along with the entire world now totally isolated and trapped, imprisoned in our homes by what was called the Coronavirus, Covid-19, and many other names along the way. It's one thing to stay home because you want to, but hiding from an unknown germ that could put you on a respirator, separate you from your loved ones, and even take your life, created a whole new perspective on simply trying to survive.

It was hard to find joy in those early spring mornings as we listened to the news and watched the death toll climb. Fear, sadness, and uncertainty quietly moaned throughout the land as everyone tried to cope. The world was upside down and we were all hanging on together. When we could no longer deny what was happening, we devised a system of gathering necessary supplies and securing toilet paper, which was the first staple to be in shortage.

Food became our next challenge. How were we going to purchase our groceries without leaving home? And, like the toilet paper, would there be any staples left on the shelves for us to buy? Three months later, with our new survival system finally in place, we now found ourselves bored. To solve that problem, my friend and I became master chefs of the kitchen, indulging in our favorite buffet of foods daily. Of course, indulging in all these homemade treats and taking many more naps than necessary, it soon became obvious we would probably succumb to isolation if we didn't find a way to bring purpose and some type of meaning back into our lives.

We continued to social distance, which meant staying away from everyone, and sought ways to change our situation. With each creative idea, there always seemed to be some form of risk attached and we questioned, "Would this venture be worth dying for?" and the idea was soon forgotten.

What was about to become the adventure of our lifetime started the day I first noticed an invitation to enter my favorite photo in a magazine contest. Anything to do with creativity generally grabs my attention, and this was no exception. After debating my skills and picture-taking ability, the excitement had already moved in and I justified my rash decision with, "Well, this would be a fun venture and we can isolate in our vehicle."

I had a little pocket camera that had been purchased just a few months earlier and I had no idea how to use the crazy thing. No matter; I would learn as I went. My friend and I were unstoppable. We were going to find that perfect picture and win a contest.

With the camera in hand, we were ready for the hunt. The garage door slowly opened on that very first day and a shiny bright Silverado pickup emerged. It was a brave sort, I would say, having no idea of what we were about to ask, for surely it was never going to be quite the same, and neither were these two friends.

Day one held no plan, except for packing a picnic lunch. I grabbed a bottle of water, my camera, and my very old flip phone, and off we went. Deciding where to go first was the hardest part of our day. After some serious discussion, we soon found ourselves heading south of Sioux Falls wandering from one country road to the next, driving through the beautiful rolling hills of the Sioux Valley. This scenic drive was surrounded by rich farmland and abundant crops with a few little towns sprinkled along the way. It was a peaceful drive that welcomed us. It reflected remnants from the past along with all the wonders of the present, and our memories were awakened!

Having grown up on a farm, touring the countryside seemed like the natural thing to do. However, choosing to become an explorer at our age was not an easy task. Our legs were wobbly, the ditches steep, and poor vision took its toll, especially with my small camera and those pesky bugs. At times it definitely was not much fun! To make a long story short, six months and 1,600 photos later I had a little better feel for my camera, but now what about all those photos?

After filling the camera and putting the dusty dirty Silverado to bed each night, we would review our treasures and wonder if we had captured the prize. We were smitten! Something was going on—perhaps it was all the bug bites—but we were being compelled to continue this massive photo hunt.

Covid-19 had shut everything down. If we were lucky enough to find an open gas station, we were not going to risk our lives going in for a snack—mask or no mask! To pump gas we wore disposable gloves followed by lots of hand sanitizer. To add an extra measure of protection, we carried a bucket of soapy water along with us wherever we went. By now you are probably wondering about using bathrooms. All I can say is, being raised on the farm, we were well trained in this area. Things had not changed much according to the isolation protocol. We were still in lock-down, simply switching our location from staying home to isolating on long drives in the country.

After our first few unplanned trips, we both agreed to set a fifty-mile radius around the city of Sioux Falls and limit our outings to a few hours each week in a little more organized plan that would eventually lead us through most of the southeastern corner of South Dakota.

Despite the pandemic and all the sorrow and sadness that surrounded us, we were smiling again. But why were we smiling when the rest of the world was feeling so much pain? Our thoughts began moving us in a new direction and we noticed our focus starting to change. It was no longer about winning a photo contest. Sure, that idea was probably still floating around in the back of our minds, but the focus was now on the happiness we were feeling and how all this excitement and wonder could be shared with others.

We explored each community, gathering our ideas and learning from our mistakes—and believe me, we had many. With plenty of time to think on this subject eventually, we came up with an idea. We would follow our explorations and create the perfect day trip. Initially, without a plan and GPS tech support, we were all over the countryside, often visiting many small towns more than once. There was nothing wrong with return visits; it meant more fun and finding treasures missed the first time. But if we were going to create this perfect day trip we needed to be more organized.

Continuing in our journey, it became very evident that each community held a vast array of history, treasures, and charm. What we were finding was much more than a simple day trip. Our trip was power, intrigue, and excitement that grew into *The Ten Trails of the Heartland.*

Tidbit Treats will acquaint and stir the appetite of each explorer. "You-can't-eat-just-one" snacks will always keep you wanting more, and so it is with this rich southeastern South Dakota history.

This was the first outing. We were living in the moment and having a great time with an occasional photo captured along the way. Prior to this day, trips in and out of each community were done with shallow vision; looking, but not really seeing. This time, we were leaving footprints, and deliberately seeking more. We were hungry for each gravel road and where it would lead next. Unknown to us, a much greater journey lay ahead. Lessons were waiting and determination was ready to lead us to this thing called joy.

Tidbits & Photo Hunt

Don't forget to search for the big red heart hidden in plain sight in each of the following towns!

CANTON

Canton, our first stop, is one of the oldest communities in what was known as Dakota Territory before South Dakota became a state in 1889. It is the county seat for Lincoln County and was originally known as Gate City for many years before it was officially named Canton. In 1925 Canton was selected as the site for the National Ski Tournament hosting over 10,000 fans, and again in 1930 held its second National Tournament.
www.cantonsd.org

Mural "Imagine" a colorful, vibrant work conveying a message of diversity and beauty. Artist Dave Fuller, Parker, SD

FAIRVIEW

1

Fairview is a small town in Lincoln County, laid out in 1886 and named after the scenic views of the surrounding Sioux Valley. Your visit to Fairview and peaceful drive through the valley will fill your day with warm memories. Be sure and check out the Fairview Greenhouse, a sure delight for garden lovers. www.davedaale.com/Roni.html

2

HUDSON

1

Hudson is the easternmost community in South Dakota, named in 1868 by a group of early settlers from Hudson, Iowa. Amanda Clement became a Hudson celebrity when she came to be the first woman to work for pay as a baseball umpire. Hudson Meats and Sausage is one of those places where you will find tasty treasures to take home with you. www.hudsonmeats.org

2

ALCESTER

Alcester was founded in 1879 in what was then called Cole County. The county was later renamed Union County. In 1921 DeeCort Hammitt became the director of the Alcester Community Band. Seven years later, when the summer White House was located in the Black Hills, his band played for President Calvin Coolidge. In 1943 Hammitt composed "Hail South Dakota" which was chosen as South Dakota's state song.

www.alcestersd.org

1

2

3

4

5

NORA

Nora, once a community with two stores—a blacksmith shop and a creamery—now boasts a population of five. During December, this tiny little community comes alive with Christmas tradition! Since 1989 people continue to come from far and wide to enjoy the sounds of the beautiful pipe organ and sing Christmas carols in the middle of a nostalgic country store. A priceless experience that is not to be missed! www.facebook.com/norasouthdakota

BERESFORD

BERESFORD is a city in Lincoln and Union County. It was originally called Paris in 1873, and renamed in 1884 after Lord Charles Beresford. Beresford is very near to the center of the North American continent, being far removed from any large bodies of water. You will find a beautiful treasured library in Beresford with over 30,000 items. www.beresfordsd.com

"Evening Shadows the Land", artists Mary Wick and Edward Raventon, 1996

NORWAY CENTER

Norway Center was first established by Norwegian and Swedish settlers as Moe Township. In 1927, they built their dreams and hopes for the future on a railroad that would never come through. A store and township hall is all that survived. Nonetheless, the little township hall across from the store became the powerful pathway to the South Dakota State House, where seven legislators and one governor—Archie Gubrud (1961-65)—started their political careers.

NEWTON HILLS STATE PARK

LAKE LAKOTA

LAKE LAKOTA
PATTEE CREEK WATERSHED PROJECT
FOR FLOOD PREVENTION & RECREATION
WATER SURFACE AREA - 90 ACRES
RECREATION-STORAGE-1,110 AC. FT.
FLOODWATER-STORAGE-930 AC. FT.
DRAINAGE AREA - 8.9 SQ MILES
HEIGHT OF DAM - 43 FEET
VOLUME OF FILL-155,000 CU.YDS

ROLLINGS GAME PRODUCTION AREA HUDSON

Sioux Valley Trail
Legacy Love Notes

On (date):____________ I found the hearts at: __________________

What I like the most was: ______________________________

Joy From the Trip

Heartland Trail

CHAPTER 2

HEARTLAND TRAIL

It has been over fifty years since that gentle tear rolled down my cheek and goodbye was said. The farm had been the most important place in my life, a haven of wonder and curiosity. I spent hours building secret forts in the tall weeds and wondered why my eyes were itching. I watched butterflies float through the sky, and thought to myself, *How do they do that*? Curled in the grass watching the clouds dance in the sky I felt the warmth of the summer sun and, of course, played the game, "What Shape Am I Now?"

With each summer that would come and go, the days filled with wonder and curiosity seemed to fade with the sunset. Time passes quickly but childhood memories linger on. At times we grab at the past, and click our heels together, quietly whispering, "I want to go home, I want to go home." But just as the butterfly floats through our lives, so go the thoughts of home.

On one of our early trips, we decided to venture into areas less known to us. Of course, not having a plan, we would head wherever the moment led. Without a smartphone or GPS system, we were on our own. Having lived around the Sioux Falls region for many years, the word "lost" was not in our vocabulary.

We packed a wonderful lunch and decided to have a picnic on the shore of a little lake we had stumbled upon several years ago. For some reason, on this particular day, we were excited and decided to hit the road early, which was highly unusual for us. Heading south from Sioux Falls, we followed a lovely winding back road which took us through a beautiful river valley. It was an unforgettable summer morning. The birds were singing, frogs croaking, and we were feeling freedom—something we had not felt for a long time. After all these years, those peaceful, happy moments that I had so longed for since my childhood had returned.

Jumping out to snap each photo, my memory took me back to the ditches I used to walk, the flowering thistles my dad simply hated, black dirt in my shoes, cattle quietly grazing the fields, and the heat of the noonday sun. I was home.

Euphoric feelings filled the cab of our pickup and mixed with the gentle breezes from our open windows. Freedom was in the air. What we take for granted each day can slip away so quickly. We both knew we were being given a second chance in this land we call God's Country.

It was noon and we were getting hungry. We had been driving gravel roads all morning and now circling the area where we thought the lake should be. We weren't lost—misplaced perhaps—but we were not finding this mysterious little lake. We could have moved along and enjoyed our lunch elsewhere but both of us were determined to find the lake. You need to understand we were in farm country, surrounded by beautiful crops, hayfields, and silos. What you might expect to see traveling down the

gravel roads would be a tractor or some other form of farm machinery. What did we see? A pickup pulling a very nice-sized fishing boat!

At first, we both laughed. It's a mirage! But as soon as we realized this boat might lead us to the lake, we quickly followed. It had been a long five miles. We were getting hungry and eating this guy's dust from the dry gravel road was not satisfying the hunger. The chase now continued down a highway, and at this point, we began wondering if we were being led astray, as we knew this road would eventually

end up at the Missouri River where you would probably find many other boats such as this. After another four miles of quiet doubt and thinking maybe we should just give up, the pickup and boat suddenly turned, taking a new direction. At that moment there was wild excitement. We knew we had found the lake.

After this brief detour and many moments of wonder, we were again under the warm summer sun and beautiful blue sky, sitting on the shore of this elusive little lake, laughing, giggling, and enjoying our lunch. For many, this may be called a coincidence, but we knew we were not alone; we had a guide for this journey.

Covid-19 was still on the prowl. During the early days of the pandemic, people were hiding. The world was closed, and only essential places such as grocery stores, gas stations, and hospitals were open and things felt abnormally strange. You might occasionally see someone out on the streets, but most of the time each community felt like a ghost town.

Windows were the spoken voice from those sheltering in place. Many were lavishly decorated with hearts, teddy bears, and various messages. We all felt the pain; not one person was exempt. There was no denying it; we were all in this together! The only positive note was that we had the roads to ourselves, but it simply wasn't as much fun without people. The hunt was on. Block by block as though we had just lost our pet puppy, we searched home after home, business after business, every main street, playground, health facility, water tower, and school, stopping occasionally to read a poster. We were intrigued with the beauty of each church and the ruggedness of the grain elevators, both on quiet watch over their town.

On this particular day, my driver calmly listened as I explained, "My memories are having an anxiety attack." He gave me a strange look and kept driving. How was he to answer that statement? This was my explanation. Over the years, I had the fortune or misfortune of moving numerous times, more than I even care to think about. Each move brought me to a new home, new surroundings, and new communities to love and enjoy. I was back in those moments feeling homesick, a feeling I had come to know well. I needed to convince myself this was not about moving—at least for the moment. Memories calmed, my driver scratched his head a little and quietly kept driving.

With each intense search came questions: "Why was this color chosen?"; "How did each city street get its name?"; "Why is there a barn in the middle of town?" Wonder had come alive, and it followed us everywhere! We sensed our guide encouraging us to move along. We had eight trails yet to explore, and wonder chattered, "Where do we go next?"; and "What are we going to find?"

Don't forget to search for the big red heart hidden in plain sight in each of the following towns!

HURLEY

Hurley is known as "the small town with a big heart." In its early beginnings, it was named after R.E. Hurley, a railroad engineer. Each year Hurley celebrates "Hot Hurley Nights," a weekend of exciting, down-home, fun-filled entertainment. www.hurleysd.com

"Some Gave All" etched on the Veterans Memorial, Hurley SD

VIBORG

Viborg was known in the early 1860s as Daneville. "Danish Days" is a celebration of heritage that brings the "Aebleskiver" (round Danish pancake) back into town every year. While visiting be sure and stop at the Daneville Heritage Museum, an experience not to be missed! www.viborgsd.org

1

2

3

4

5

IRENE

Irene shares its location with three different counties and is referred to as "The Village in the Valley." It has been the home of the Irene Rodeo for over 26 years; home of the Irene/Wakonda Eagles; and home of 2018 Miss South Dakota, Lexy Schenk. www.irenesd.com

"Freedom Isn't Free!" painted by the late Greg Preheim, Irene

CENTERVILLE

Centerville, in the early beginnings, found itself in the center of two well-traveled trails, those of the stagecoach and the US mail. On the west side of town on the banks of the Vermillion River, a large flour mill served the community well until it was lost to fire in 1930. Gunderson Park claimed the title "The Beach," as people far and wide flocked to enjoy swimming, water slides, the concession stand, and picnics. Tornado Days is the community celebration held each year over the Fourth of July weekend and features toilet bowl races, golf tournaments, softball games, fun, and excitement for everyone.
www.centervillesd.com

DAVIS

Davis is a small town with a population of 85, according to the 2010 census. In 1920 it was a much larger town, with a population of 245. In 1928 Davis fell victim to a massive tornado that injured over half the people. Davis may appear small but excels in creativity and charm and is a delight not to be missed. While there, be sure to check out the Solace Farm General Store, "a shopping experience with a look into the past." www.solacefarm.net

State Parks & Recreational Areas

SWAN LAKE

Swan Lake Christian Camp
SLCC

GUNDERSON PARK, CENTERVILLE

Heartland Trail Legacy Love Notes

On (date):__________ I found the hearts at: ________________

____

____

What I like the most was: __________________________________

____

Joy From the Trip

____

____

____

____

____

____

____

____

____

____

Wetland Trail

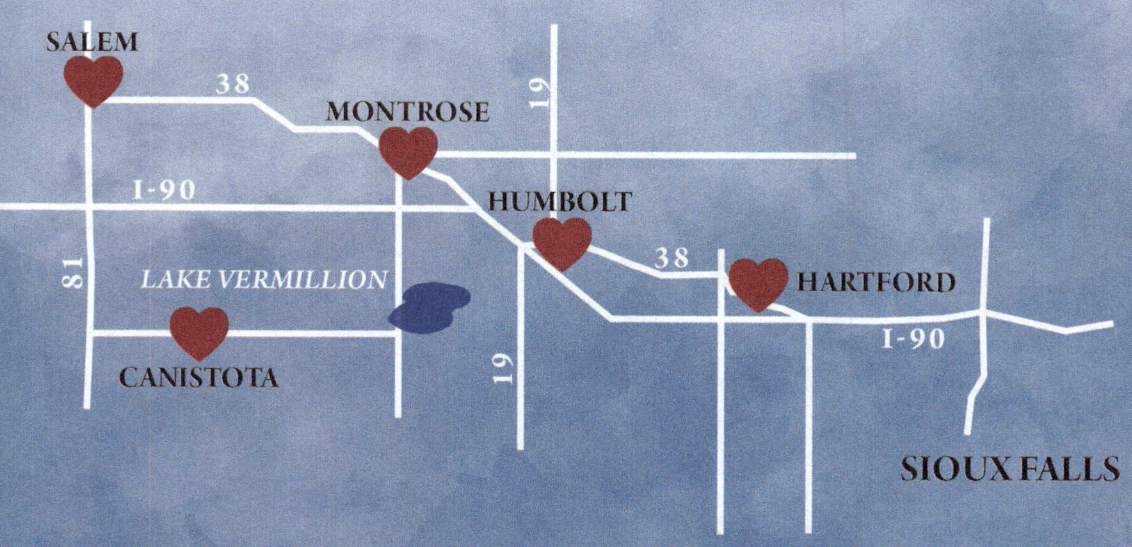

CHAPTER 3

WETLAND TRAIL

Pothole paradise, wildlife production areas, and farming, all woven together, definitely give us a picture of what has been known for years: South Dakota is a land of infinite variety.

Farming around and through wetlands can be quite a challenge, but somehow the farmers manage to pull it off. Where you find water preventing the planting of crops, there you may find cattle quietly grazing the land. For such an accomplished feat, these farmers have the blessings of living smack-dab in the middle of great areas of hunting, fishing, birding, and recreational boating. You can't beat that!

Early well-known explorers Lewis and Clark traveled through this Dakota Territory in pairs, and that idea is still great wisdom for today. Most of the country's back roads are very well kept and a joy to travel, but occasionally, you will find areas of caution. We were always ready for the unexpected, bringing a blanket, extra jackets, rain gear, insect repellant, a flashlight, sandwiches, and

bottled water. And, of course, our modern-day rescue tool, the cell phone, just in case we found ourselves in trouble after venturing onto one of these strange roads.

A movie released in 1989 tells the story of a 74-year-old widow and the chauffeur hired by her son. I had forgotten this movie, but it quickly came to mind when my friend asked, "Where would you like to go next, Miss Kelley?" Well, that stuck! We were now officially "Driver" and "Miss Kelley."

After spending hours together in the front seat of the pickup, we were not only exploring the rural countryside, but also were learning more and more about each other's strange quirks. With each of us having only one working ear—his right and my left—we were never quite certain of what the other had just said. Of course, our lack of hearing and making assumptions did create a few dramatic moments. But despite most of our old age imperfections, we were still a great pair.

During our early beginnings, my driver was just that, my driver, and all these photo stops were interrupting his quiet ride. From that perspective, each photo opportunity became a timed event. Leaping out of the pickup to grab a photo, I found I had only two minutes and maybe two quick shots before the motor roared or the horn gave a sudden beep. That was it; time to move on. I quickly adapted and became more selective in my photo choices. I think it is called compromise. To my amazement, and only by the grace of God, I never lost a shot. Usually, that quickly grabbed photo was a keeper.

Some photos were unusual, and others simply fun, like the picture of the cattle on page seventy-one. Growing up on the farm and spending many moments with animals, I had some understanding of their unique behaviors. I calmly slipped out of the pickup that day and approached the curious cattle. As you may notice, I had their full attention, grabbing that first shot when suddenly, "Yee-haw! Yee-haw!" loudly rang out from the cab of our truck. Any additional shots were gone, along with the cattle.

With each photo op, laughter and happiness filled the air. This was something we had not felt for quite some time, and with all our excitement we captured more interesting photos than we ever expected. We were smitten. It seems you can never get enough happiness when you find it.

Most days, the weather was warm and sunny, and it was wonderful to bask in the peaceful moments. There were no radios, television, or Smartphone distractions; it was simply the two of us, like a pair of clouds in the sky, floating peacefully along. This was our time. We had no set agenda and no particular place to be.

Covid -19 was still hovering, and we were doing our best to ignore it. We found many intriguing shops and restaurants we would normally have stopped to enjoy if everything hadn't been closed. Brief moments of sadness tried to creep back into our lives. But we silently forged ahead and prayed all this unbelievable madness would eventually end, and the world would again be ours.

Creativity could be found within each community. Some displayed it boldly, while others maintained more reserve, but it was still there. Being a creative person, I love handcrafted works, and my camera was now becoming my canvas and dearest friend. There was always surprise and jubilation when we found another treasure; the more eye-catching, the more excitement of the moment. We never

knew what surprise would be discovered next. We were experiencing the thrill of the hunt.

One afternoon, we pulled into a nature area expecting to see perhaps a fisherman, some waterfowl, or beautiful habitat. But instead, waiting for us under the protection and loving arms of a very old oak tree sat a velvet couch. It was a beautiful sight sitting gracefully in the arms of Mother Nature. "Come sit for a spell," it whispered. Our wonder was awakened.

Moment by moment along these vast gravel roads, an occasional discouraging thought would appear, tempting us. *Just ignore this little town; you will never find a treasure here.* We paid no attention to those negative thoughts. Since both of us love a good challenge, the battle

was on. "Miss Kelley" and her driver were not leaving town until a treasured photo was found.

This intense search brought us to a greater awareness of each unique community. During those moments of negativity, we learned to refocus and take a closer look. Not everything was in plain sight. This would take more persistence and determination on our part. But we knew there would be excitement and joy when the treasure was finally found. Just when we thought we might fail, we turned around and began searching in the opposite direction, this time with success. The treasure had been there all along.

We realized continuing in the same direction would often bring missed opportunities, and many times corrections and adjustments were necessary before we were able to see the whole picture. The same is true with our lives. Often the greatest blessings are hidden. Persistence will keep us on the path and happiness will be our reward.

We were having a good time. Smiles and even tears of joy began filling our souls once again. Wonder was blazing the trail, and curiosity brought happiness. But difficulties were also an ever-present danger as we forged ahead. Would we have the strength and determination to blaze those more difficult trails yet to come?

Tidbits & Photo Hunt

Don't forget to search for the big red heart hidden in plain sight in each of the following towns!

HARTFORD

Hartford was settled in 1878 and named Oakville after its first early settler E.I. Oakes. Its motto is "On the edge of everything." Jamboree Days and Hartford Hometown Christmas are exciting yearly events for all. www.hartfordsd.us

Mural artists: Amber Hansen, Darcy Millette, and the Community of Hartford

4

5

HUMBOLDT

Humboldt, off interstate 90 at exit 379, marks the halfway point on the longest interstate in the U.S. and proudly claims the title of the highest point of elevation between the Missouri and Mississippi rivers. It was first settled in 1877 and named in 1880 to honor Baron Alexander Von Humboldt, a German naturalist, botanist and scientist. Each year this "small town with a big heart" celebrates the harvest season with an old-fashioned threshing show. www.humboldt.govoffice.com

2

1

3

MONTROSE

Montrose, located along the bank of the "East Vermillion River, had its beginning in 1880 when it was platted and named. The northern area surrounding this charming little town is known as Pleasant Valley, and its name reflects just that. Be sure and plan extra time to explore this community and enjoy the beauty of this peaceful valley.
www.cityofmontrosesd.com

1

2

3

SALEM

Salem at one time shared the same name as another community. To solve this problem its name was changed to Melas, which is Salem spelled backward. It eventually reclaimed its original name when the other community was no more. Salem is the county seat for McCook County. Its motto is, "A city to grow in." www.salemsd.com

2

1

3

CANISTOTA

Canistota was chosen and established to become a railroad community in 1883. Since 1915 the long-standing Ortman Chiropractic Clinic has called Canistota home and attracted people from every state in the U.S.
www.canistotasd.com

State Parks & Recreational Areas

LAKE VERMILLION STATE RECREATION AREA

Wetland Trail
Legacy Love Notes

On (date):____________ I found the hearts at: __________________

____

____

What I like the most was: _____________________________________

____

Joy From the Trip

____

____

____

____

____

____

____

____

____

____

Big Sioux River Trail

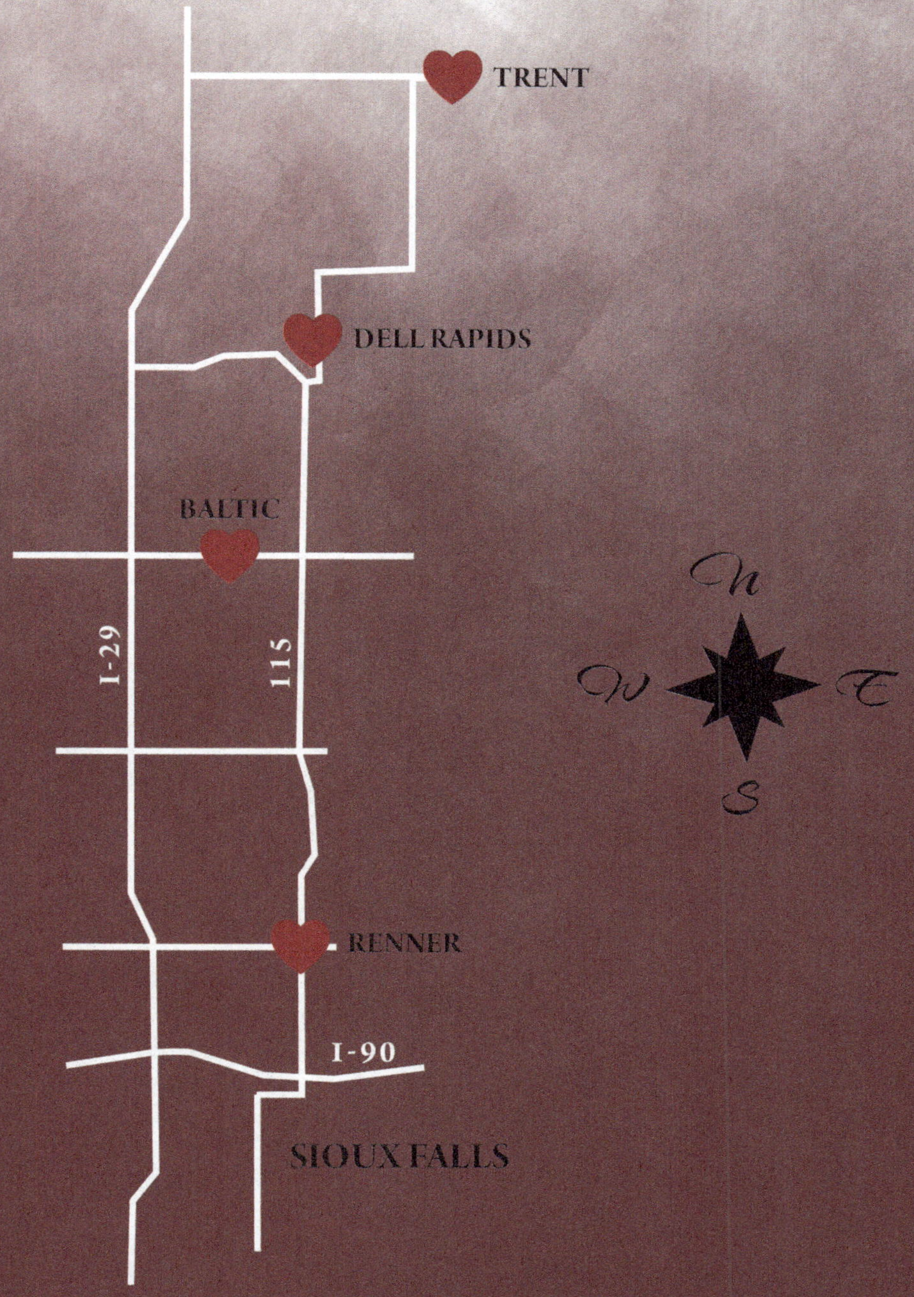

CHAPTER 4

BIG SIOUX RIVER TRAIL

From its amazingly humble beginnings, the Big Sioux River carried the water of life and forged its way through pillars of quartzite, a rock that was third only to the strength of diamonds. Its first people recognized the opportunities it offered, and this spirit of enthusiasm brought strength and hope for all.

Struggles came hard and fast to each new settlement. Floods, storms, raging fires, drought, and crop-eating insects did everything they could to destroy those early dreams. With strength from above and wisdom as their guide, the people continued their journey, utilizing what they found right in their back yard—quartzite. With it, they created beautiful architectural wonders that had been made to last.

Most of us have had struggles, large or small, in our lives, and it was no different for Miss Kelley and her driver. We were now the older generation and probably needed to act our age. But in truth, sometimes finding ourselves in circumstances beyond our control or suddenly discovering an exciting treasure, we did get a little noisy.

With the mindset of a spring chick, I could leap out of the pickup and madly chase down each photo. But upon my return, I now found myself to be this grandma who didn't bend as easy, and getting back into the pickup was a real struggle. With these short little legs and a few extra pounds due to Covid, my driver, bless his heart, would grab my hand and try his best to pull me back in, which was no easy feat and probably would have made another great picture.

Trying to operate my new camera gave me a few challenges. Honestly, I had no idea what I was doing, but I was giving it my all! I remember the old saying, "She's as blind as a bat." I had now become that bat. The viewfinder on my camera seemed to be quite small for my eyes, and it was anybody's guess what I was framing. Many times I just said a quick prayer and aimed. I suspected prayers were also going on behind the steering wheel as my driver held his breath, watching me teeter on the edge of many ditches. With my hands flying through the air like an acrobat, I was putting on quite a show. And going to the emergency room was not an option!

On one occasion, an unknown hitchhiker joined our party. My first suspicion came after arriving home when suddenly the itching began. A thorough exam had now led me to my hair. Suddenly this creepy bug jumped out, and just like that was gone, but not before doing his damage. I still question how one bug could raise so much havoc. Anyway, for the next three weeks, anti-itch lotion became my new attire. Looking a little rough and somewhat out of sorts, for the first time, I was glad to be in isolation and social distancing.

It had been a tough summer thus far for the entire world, and it was now the 4th of July weekend, a time for picnics and families, swimming, boating, parades, and exciting fireworks displays. Instead, everything was closed and canceled!

People needed people, and they needed their families. Our friends and family disappeared like a puff of smoke. Everyone was in isolation. We were together in spirit but still alone. Despite the pandemic and total isolation, we were still led to new friends. We called them our "trail angels," a term of endearment given to people who have provided kindness and generosity to those in need along their journey.

On this particular warm summer day, we were deeply entrenched into this small community, searching madly for our next treasured photo when we discovered a most intriguing home. Creativity was spilling everywhere. Glorious colors flowed like a river, and banks of flowers were calling my name. The owners just happened to be in their yard when I jumped out, asking if I could take a few pictures. I started snapping photo after photo, definitely in my element, when they asked us to join in a treat. It was National Root Beer Float

Day! Now, how could we turn down that request?

Soon we were enjoying this most refreshing beverage in an old vintage corn crib, wonderfully transformed into a summer man cave. Everything had been set up so cleverly, including a little outhouse that seemed to be peeking through the flowerbed. We spent the rest of that afternoon like four long-lost friends soaking in every piece of eye candy, sharing laughter, life's many experiences, and fun! Not only did we discover wonderful photos, but we also found new friends.

Just as we were doing, people everywhere were also trying to break the bonds of isolation, creating whatever sense of freedom worked for them. Designs of hope and love began filling windows, storefronts, and lawns. Car parades were organized to celebrate birthdays, anniversaries, and weddings. People stood on street corners playing trumpets or horns of various types, entertaining those neighbors who bravely ventured onto their front porch.

Driver and Miss Kelley were still enjoying the countryside, and as all farmers do, we were also checking crops. The corn was doing especially well according to the farmer's standard measure, knee-high by the 4th of July.

During the long drives, we would occasionally compare moments in our past, realizing we had both at one time or another driven through or had some involvement with many of these small towns. Some we knew well and others not at all. On one occasion during our travels, we accidentally entered one of our better-known towns from a new direction, realizing a new treasure we had never known before.

It was a familiar path we had always followed, the one that came easy, felt comfortable, and led us to wherever we thought we needed to be. With this discovery, we found ourselves feeling sad, knowing we had missed years of enjoyment, but we also realized we had a second chance to enjoy this blessing.

This country is no stranger to struggles, and we have all had our share. Sometimes the road is comfortable and easy to follow; other times we find it full of potholes and sharp turns that will challenge our very being. We may choose to follow the easier path or miss the better road entirely. Keep searching and never give up! The right path is out there and will bring joy and happiness when discovered.

The people along the Big Sioux River Trail took each negative moment and gained wisdom. They took the ashes in their lives and found a new path, one of strength and determination. They were willing to try again.

We were still in the early stages of this journey. Full of wonder, excitement, and renewed strength, we were ready to blaze a new trail. Looking ahead, we noticed many intriguing paths. Which one would be our next choice?

Don't forget to search for the big red heart hidden in plain sight in each of the following towns!

RENNER

Renner was founded in 1898. In May 1927, after completing the first solo non-stop flight across the Atlantic Ocean, Charles Lindberg paid a visit to Renner, where thousands of people flocked to this little town in celebration of their new hero. In the 1930's Renner corner became one of the busiest areas around. Today it continues that tradition with a fresh meat market and restaurant for all to enjoy.
www.rennercorner.com

BALTIC

Baltic was originally named St. Olaf in 1981, Keyes in 1887, and Baltic in 1889. The Baltic Centennial was celebrated, 1881-1981, and today gladly shares those 100 years of history with all.
www.baltic.govoffice.com

DELL RAPIDS

Dell Rapids was built in 1868 and was originally known as Dell City. When fire destroyed most of the town in the 1880s, the new community was made to last. Local quarries provided rose quartzite, and architectural beauties came to life. Today Dell Rapids carries the motto, "The little city with the big attractions."
www.cityofdellrapids.org

TRENT

Trent was laid out in 1874, and today is filled with nostalgia, history, and small-town charm. Just outside of town, "The Little Village Farm" turned museum, is a must-see attraction offering collections of rural South Dakota windmills, farm sheds, antiques, and 7,200 seed corn farming caps. A great photo stop!

2

3

1

4

State Parks & Recreational Areas

RIVER PARK BALTIC

SIOUX RIVER RED ROCK TRAIL DELL RAPIDS

DELL RAPIDS CITY PARK

HISTORIC BATHHOUSE

DELLS OF THE SIOUX RECREATION AREA

Big Sioux River Trail
Legacy Love Notes

On (date):__________ I found the hearts at: ______________

____

____

What I like the most was: ____________________________

____

Joy From the Trip

____

____

____

____

____

____

____

____

____

____

Old West Trail

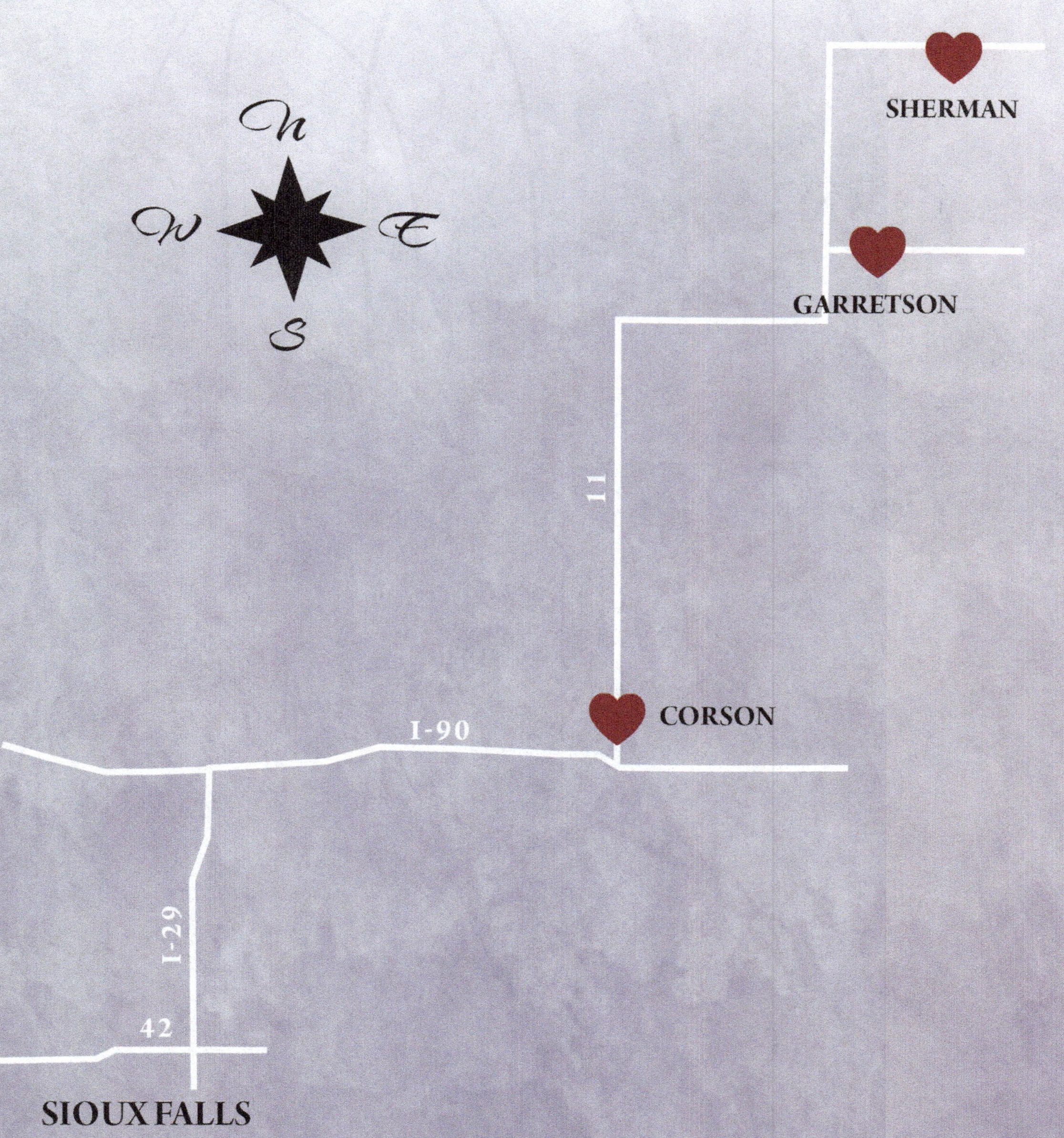

CHAPTER 5

OLD WEST TRAIL

Rugged meets beauty, wonder brings excitement, the transition from old to new begins. Covered wagons loaded with hope and dreams filled the countryside, claims were staked, railroads arrived, and soon little towns seemed to magically appear on the horizon. Opportunity flowed like a river, capturing the interest of many, eventually setting the stage for saddlebags full of rich history.

In the middle of all this commotion, Splitrock Creek became a respite for all, winding through stately eruptions of quartzite, lending calm reverence and beauty to the rural countryside. Occasionally, this quiet serenity would be interrupted with out-of-control life happenings, such as the day alleged bank robber, Jesse James escaped capture by jumping, horseback, over Devils Gulch.

Mural artist Jill Fedders-Ellefson, Sherman, SD

Sometimes curiosity takes us in a new direction, but most of the time, we take control. This particular day started in a rather boring fashion. As my kids would say, "Mom's having a bad hair day."

I felt like my driver was not going in the direction we should be going (whatever direction that was), but I also knew sometimes he didn't know where we were going and simply didn't care. So I thought to myself, *Why am I making this a big deal? I need to just sit back, relax, and enjoy the trip.*

Soon we noticed something interesting: a crop-spraying helicopter. We had never seen this before, as most crop sprayers we knew of were small, specifically designed planes. We watched intently as the pilot maneuvered around and under the huge power lines that blocked his path, most of the time coming within a few feet from the ground to avoid the power lines above. This was quite a performance, one that we would have missed had I insisted on going my way.

Over the last two months, we had already driven past hundreds of farms and had a good idea of what to expect: a home, barn, silo or two, various forms of farm equipment, and, of course, animals. After the helicopter performance, we continued for another couple of miles when I suddenly yelled, "Stop!" I could not believe my eyes! This was not the norm, and I kept yelling, "Stop! There's a fighter jet on that farm." My driver—bless his heart—thought I was having delusions, answered, "I don't see any fighter jet."

After some exploration into this unusual finding, the farmer and his sons shared their wonderful story. According to these very excited young men, their grandfather had flown this South Dakota fighter jet in 1952. Excitedly, they continued their story as they walked me to what had now become their jet, proudly sitting in the cockpit or standing on the wing as I snapped each photo. As the story goes, over the years this plane has touched many hearts, young and old alike, and gathered quite a following. Grandpa's jet had finally come home. What a heart-warming moment! I can only imagine in a few years where those fine young men will be.

Benton Howe stands on the wing of the F89 Scorpion his grandfather flew in 1952.

Masks were becoming a huge deal in our fight against Covid. We were told as long as we respected the six-foot social distancing protocol and wore masks, we would probably be somewhat safe. Soon, masks were cropping up everywhere, as creative entrepreneurs hacked their wares from the street corners and markets.

My sister became the mask maker in our family and provided us with fashionable protection fit for every occasion. My daily facial moments became very brief and it no longer mattered how much "beauty" I put on my face. No one was going to see it anyway, so with a little eye magic, I was ready for another day in captivity.

Over the years, I have learned that wearing some type of costume usually propels me into a new identity. And, as actors would say, you are then to "assume the role." I must confess, I probably took this

advice a little too seriously. The first time I tried on my mask, I felt like robbing a bank (go figure). Perhaps it would have been better for Jesse James to never have put on a mask.

Driver and Miss Kelley were still acclimating to this new life. Sometimes we experienced minor power struggles, but nothing a kind word didn't resolve. He focused on his quiet, peaceful drive, as I obsessively looked for the next exciting photo.

We were not exactly on the same page, but we were trying. One afternoon, after spotting some really fun camera shots, Miss Kelley was feeling the excitement of the moment, wildly snapping photos that caught her eye. Eventually, returning to the pickup happily out of breath, her driver asked, "Did you snap one of BigFoot?"

My response was, "Where?" To make a long story short, as you can see, that interesting photo is now part of our collection. My joy was contagious. We were finally on the same page. If you consider madly trying to outdo each other to be a team effort, then we had even become a team.

There are always choices to be made in the prairies and valleys of life, some good and some bad. Since the beginning of time, everyone began life's journey on a path filled with choices. In staking their claims in this new territory, some were given rags that ended in riches, while others were blessed with opportunity and wealth, only to cross the finish line with nothing.

Driver and Miss Kelley were not exempt. Each day we, too, had many choices to make. On this particular day, it was to control or not control, and always thinking of the good of others became the right choice. We were ready to move on as a team.

This marathon was ours, and we were well on the way to achieving our goal. We were both tough challengers, and the bar had been set. Wonder was loudly questioning, "Who will be the winner of this battle?"

Tidbits & Photo Hunt

Don't forget to search for the big red heart hidden in plain sight in each of the following towns!

CORSON

Corson is a small, unincorporated community that links local farming and industry to the railroad system. Henry Tabor Corson brought promise, influence, and his name into the community when he successfully linked the rail service from Corson to Sioux Falls.

3

1

4

2

GARRETSON

Garretson was first known as Garretson City. It was originally settled in 1872, two miles south of its present location in the area known today as the Palisades State Park. This little town gained its notoriety after a bank robbery in North Field, MN when alleged bank robber Jesse James escaped a posse after leaping Devil's Gulch on horseback.

www.cityofgarretson.com

Garretson School's mascot mural, by artist Jill Fedders-Ellefson, Sherman, SD

SHERMAN

Sherman sprang to life in 1888 when Edwin Sherman brought the railroad to town. Sherman was prosperous, with five grain elevators and a stock-yard, and became known throughout as a town of sophistication. Before his fame, Lawrence Welk and his band would often play for the local dances. www.shermansdak.com

State Parks & Recreational Areas

PALISADES STATE PARK

DEVIL'S GULCH AND SPLITROCK PARK, GARRETSON

Old West Trail Legacy Love Notes

On (date):__________ I found the hearts at: ______________

____

____

What I like the most was: ______________________________

____

Joy From the Trip

____

____

____

____

____

____

____

____

____

____

Farmland Trail

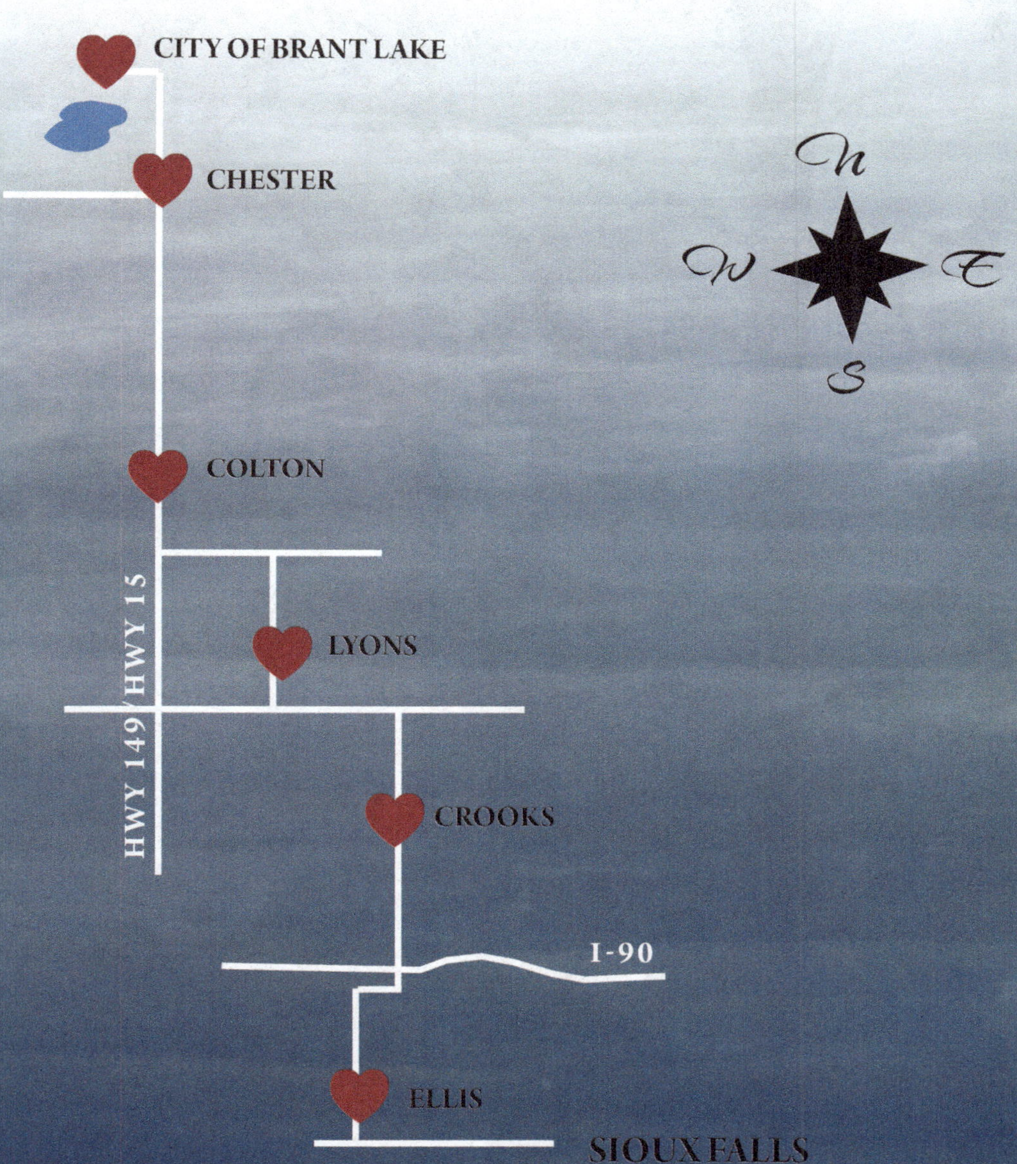

CHAPTER 6

FARMLAND TRAIL

"The color red represents an explosion of definitions, such as strength, leadership, courage, and determination, just to name a few." As I grouped this trail, my attention was immediately drawn to a color that was dominating almost every picture. You guessed it—red!

I remember my dad's farm. It was a beauty. The barn and every building in between, even down to the tiniest sheds, were painted bright red with white trim. This eye-popping testimony has held strong over the years and continues to proclaim that on this land stands a hard-working, determined, and courageous farmer. The work on the farm was tedious, and as the saying goes, "went from sunup to

sundown." But I know better. The reality, for my dad, was often the work would go around the clock and consumed every part of his life and those around him.

As each early settler claimed their prized property, the little towns grew, and so did the job descriptions of the farmers. Not only were they busy farming and caring for their property, but they were also taking on other roles, such as mayors, councilmen, church elders, and builders. Some found income in other ways. This was not a bad thing; the farmers had become the strength and foundation of most communities, while the entrepreneurs brought innovation and new business into their community, some of which grew beyond expectation and eventually achieved worldwide fame.

Physical survival was essential, and early on the communities recognized their need for a plan to call up people when someone was in trouble. Red became the color of action and response. Today this plan continues, and has now become a universal symbol, as red shiny vehicles with horns blaring and lights flashing announce to all, "We need help."

One day, we were again bouncing along gravel roads, enjoying the beautiful crops and the many farms along the way, doing our best to avoid potholes; those we accidentally hit usually shook everything, including our teeth. We arrived at our destination and had just begun exploring this unique little town when my driver noticed a change with the oil pressure gauge. I was oblivious to these concerns, of course, and continued leaping in and out of the pickup snapping my favorite shots. We always tried to drive slowly and respectfully through each community without drawing a lot of attention to this strange vehicle and this old lady running up and down the street with a camera.

Suddenly, this all changed. Each time I leaped out of the truck my driver started madly roaring the engine. I ignored the first roar; I didn't find it funny. After the second roar, I asked, "What are you doing?" I still didn't understand. By the third roar, I was a little warm under the collar, but we continued. By now it seemed the entire town was watching and intent on figuring out what was going on and questioning whether we needed help, as I was also wondering.

Eventually, this sick little pickup had to go in for a tune-up. Apparently, after driving all those gravel roads, a plugged filter needed replacing. The truck doctor told us it would be an easy fix, thank goodness, but his advice for the future was that maybe we should cool it a little on the gravel roads! I wonder what he was thinking? That expert advice only lasted about a day, for we had places to go and things to see! We were off again!

It had been six months since Covid first invaded our lives and we now found ourselves feeling the heat of the battle. Many of our family and friends contracted Covid and were fighting for their lives, some winning, others losing. Funerals were deemed unsafe with most families choosing to live-stream the service. Alone with no other family members to hug, we gathered solemnly around our computer and tearfully said our goodbyes.

We continued our drives throughout the peaceful prairie. With hearts full of sadness, tears clouding our vision, and emotions riding on our shoulders, we quietly pressed on as reflections of the past swirled throughout the loneliness of the cab. Under the warm summer sun, we searched for answers and comfort wherever it could be found. At times, it was a single flower that waved from the ditch, which brought glimpses of joy. Sometimes, it was a ray of sunshine against a beautiful cloud that gave us the strength to move along.

It was a time of deep discussion and personal soul-searching, something we had put off until now. Facing reality, we questioned whether we were prepared for the ending of this life. Of course, the answer was no since we knew we had some things to do.

Our situations may seem hopeless as we experience pain, sorrow, grief, loss, devastation, but those heavy moments are not to be carried alone. Help surrounds us each day; all we need to do is ask. Remember that when difficulties surround, goodness hides in the tears and waits at each rainbow's end. Driver and Miss Kelley were even more entrenched in this journey, for we knew perseverance would again bring goodness.

During one of our earlier drives, I snapped a quick photo of a bush ripe with massive amounts of red berries. For a brief moment, the beauty of this bush had captured my attention. But it was not until I scrolled deeper to take a better look that I discovered something remarkable. This honeysuckle bush produces its berries in pairs!

Together, we were being led deeper and deeper into the heart and spirit of each community. We better understood what the farmers already knew: life would be tough, but they had help. This is God's country and that same help is there for us.

We had never given much thought to our memories. They were simply a part of our being that occasionally moved in and out of our thoughts. I was sensing a change and noticed, as we discovered each remnant of the past, the memories were becoming bolder. Our memories were preparing to grasp our attention and tell their stories.

Don't forget to search for the big red heart hidden in plain sight in each of the following towns!

ELLIS

Ellis can be found about one mile west of the Sioux Falls city limits. It is an unincorporated community that began in 1893. It was originally called Scopeville and later renamed Ellis after A.B. Ellis, a railroad employee.

1

2

CROOKS

Crooks carried the name "New Hope" until being officially platted and renamed to honor a local politician, W.A. Crooks, 1904.
www.crookssd.org

2

1

3

LYONS

1

Lyons, first laid out in 1886, was likely named after an early pioneer from Lyons Township. Before 1975, Lyons garage had been a gas station for eighty years, with two previous owners each sharing forty of those years. July 1, 1975, Harold and Helen Boer became owners of Lyons garage and created a small modest welding and vehicle repair shop. When the occasional structure fire occurred in the village there was no fire truck or organized plan of action, so they had to rely on assistance from Crooks and Colton. The people of Lyons decided they needed a fire truck. Harold, known for his welding abilities, stepped forward to build one. When finished a bright, shiny fire truck emerged, the beginning of what was to become an internationally acclaimed fire apparatus manufacturer, Rosenbauer America.

www.rosenbaueramerica.com

2

3

COLTON

Colton was homesteaded in 1878 by J.E. Colton and named in his honor. In 1897, Colton established the first cooperative creamery. The community, seeking ways to sell their wares, established what we call today Main Street.
www.coltonsd.govoffice3.com

CHESTER

Chester was laid out in 1905. It has a creek with the unique name of Skunk, which flows along the western edge of town. Just a short mile south of Chester is Bob's Custom Meats; an interesting place to visit.

1

2

3

CITY OF BRANT LAKE

City of Brant Lake, incorporated in 2016, now claims the title of town. This lake community rests on the northeast shores of Brant Lake and enjoys all the recreational activities one can only imagine.
www.brantlakecity.com

State Parks & Recreational Areas

LAKE BRANT

WOW

Farmland Trail Legacy Love Notes

On (date):__________ I found the hearts at: ______________

____

____

What I like the most was: ______________________

____

Joy From the Trip

____

____

____

____

____

____

____

____

____

____

Ageless Prairie Trail

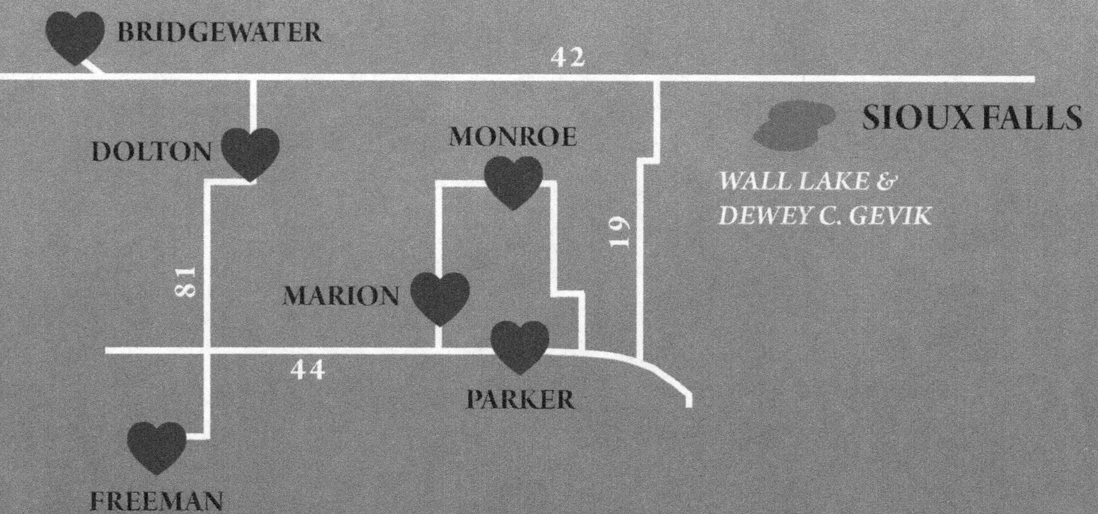

CHAPTER 7

AGELESS PRAIRIE TRAIL

They say that beauty is in the eye of the beholder. Driving through the prairie as compared to some of the other trails, one could find the roads rather boring and flat with old farm machinery, cars, and various antiques sprinkled around like salt and pepper. Where is the beauty in this picture?

When we look past the moment, we find what those who had come before envisioned: a prairie rich with opportunity, black dirt, and fertile land. Standing in vast open spaces under soft blue skies filled them with hope. They were seeing freedom...beautiful freedom. They were in *America*.

Since the beginning, the prairie has watched each generation come and go, and as the first covered wagons arrived, innovation also came to life, proudly claiming its spot in the history books. On this day, scrolling deep into my memory, emotions swelled when I caught a picture of Old Glory, a comforting term used back in my day for our great American flag, proudly standing beside each innovation introduced. Freedom and American pride had become one. Together under the bright blue skies, they have walked this prairie hand in hand, a little worn, a little tattered and torn, yet bravely they still stand, announcing to everyone, this is their land.

Miss Kelley and her driver had now become modern-day trailblazers, defined as those who forged beyond the common knowledge of their times to discover something new. We were no different from the explorers of yesteryear, except for us, the old was still new. We were definitely in our element, finding this trail packed with patriotism and acres of nostalgia. It was wonderful eye candy for our souls and healing for our hearts.

"Big Dreams Start in a Small town", mural artist Gayle Gross and her students from the Marion School District.

When the railroad first arrived, it was a big deal for those early settlers, and that remains evident today, with many towns continuing to carry the honored name of various railroad officials and their families. The railroad was instrumental in helping to lay out plans and set up rail service for each chosen community. Without this guaranteed presence of the railroad, many of the small towns would not survive.

The beautiful horizons and peaceful prairies were soon dotted with grain elevators, as trainloads of each bountiful harvest began moving through the vast prairie land toward its next destination. Later, a very similar story to that of the railroad took place when the interstate highway system plotted its course. The communities chosen to receive this service did well, while those left out—even if only by a few miles—suffered a significant loss.

Ideas and dreams filled the countryside. Those nostalgic beauties from days gone by, once praised for so much potential and celebrated grandeur, were no longer new; something better had arrived taking its place. Nostalgia began leaving a trail of memories as old quietly nestled within the prairie grass to await its future.

There was a challenge to our journey that brought newness. With each treasure found, there would be some form of excitement. At times, there was even some teasing, laughter, or wonder. We felt like children again. It didn't matter who found what first; we had discovered a way to be happy. As a result of all this fun, we were now taking more trips and staying out longer, often spending six to eight hours on the road. Once we decided to head home, we would find ourselves in disbelief, questioning how quickly time had gone by. After saying goodnight to the wonderful day and giving thanks for the Lord's protection, this pair of happily exhausted explorers gathered some much needed rest.

Covid continued to keep us in isolation, and we were missing our family, friends, and freedom. We could plan get-togethers on the patio as long as we kept the group small, wore masks, and limited our time together.

This seemed to bring some healing to our spirits, but for us, wise old owls, masks created a new set of problems by aggravating those things we were already experiencing: diminished air, compromised hearing, and muffled speech. With everyone's face covered, we couldn't read lips, and watching only the eyes, wondered what everyone was saying. There was no touching or hugs and visits were short, which was probably a good thing, as it kept the frustration minimal. All too soon, the visit was over and we were once again in hiding.

Our country drives brought freedom, and with each glimpse of nostalgia, our memories awakened to light our path. We were being taken to new places and searching thoughts we had never entertained before. Looking into the past, we were seeing happy moments, curious moments, and occasionally painful moments filled with mistakes. We recognized somthing we had taken for granted and often overlooked: the blessing of our memories, which are a treasured gift from God.

Memories are the bridge between the past, present, and future. Within a split second, our thoughts may propel us back into the exciting days of our youth when we first experienced chocolate cake, a new bike, or the thrill of driving that first car. Within another, we are whirled into the future, where we learn and make corrections from our past. Without the past, there would be no present or future.

Perhaps some of you will remember the lyrics to the popular song, "Living on Love." For our purposes, we changed the wording slightly, and "Living on Memories" became our song. Our God-given library of memories is where we can go at any moment in our lives to find hope, wisdom, strength, comfort, joy, peace, happiness, and guidance for the future.

I believe these next little thoughts to be true for most of us seniors. I probably have a little more to take care of than the rest of you, but it is of great regret that I have reached the age of, "It's time to scale back," "throw away," and "get rid of." Oh my! Those words just are not in my vocabulary!

I noticed a cartoon the other day referring to parents who absolutely cannot throw out any of their children's artwork. It depicted a support group for mothers, with one mom trying to help another, saying, "You can do this! C'mon, let me help you put that little cow in the shredder." I guess that is what we call progress, but for me, I will give thanks for every piece of old, and hold dear every ageless memory I have been given! When we remember where we started, we have the freedom to enjoy today!

We were now approaching harvest season and its beehive of activity. Wonder, curiosity, and memories packed themselves tightly into the pickup as happiness bounced all around. We were ready to go! What desires of the heart were we about to find hidden within all this hustle and bustle?

Tidbits & Photo Hunt

Don't forget to search for the big red heart hidden in plain sight in each of the following towns!

PARKER

Parker was incorporated in 1883 and is the county seat. Parker has been the host of the Turner County Fair for the last 139 years, making it the longest-running county fair in South Dakota. www.parkersd.org

2

1

MONROE

Monroe, originally called Warrington, was platted in 1887. The community may seem small but it is filled with love and charm, quietly waiting for your visit. www.monroesouthdakota.com

MARION

Marion was first named Turner Junction in 1879. Originally, this little town had two parts: Yankee Town, which was planned out by the railroad, and Russian Town, a German-speaking community. For speed enthusiasts, just outside of town, you will find "Thunder Valley Dragways," drag racing at its finest. www.marionsd.com

Larry Langerock Marion, SD

FREEMAN

Freeman is famously known for the "Schmeckfest" (festival of tasting), one of South Dakota's premier festivals, celebrating ethnic food, culture, history, and musical traditions of the community. Freeman also claims the title "Chislic Capital of America," each year proudly hosting the South Dakota Chislic Festival. www.experiencefreemansd.com

DOLTON

Dolton became a town in 1909 and was named after one of the citizens from its community. Its population listed during the 2010 census noted 37 people. Our Lady of Lourdes was a Catholic church built in Dolton and dedicated in 1908. The church building was sold in 1966, and the property was donated to the city to be used as a ball field and park.

1

2

BRIDGEWATER

Bridgewater, located in McCook County, was established in 1889. Originally called Nation, its name was changed to reflect earlier times when water was brought to town for the railroad. On February 22, 1934, Baseball Hall of Fame manager, George "Sparky" Anderson, was born in Bridgewater.
www.bridgewatersd.com

WALL LAKE

GOT
HONEY?

DEWEY C. GEVIK - OUTDOOR CONSERVATION LEARNING AREA

Ageless Prairie Trail
Legacy Love Notes

On (date):__________ I found the hearts at: ______________

____

____

What I like the most was: ______________________________

____

Joy From the Trip

____

____

____

____

____

____

____

____

____

____

Harvest Trail

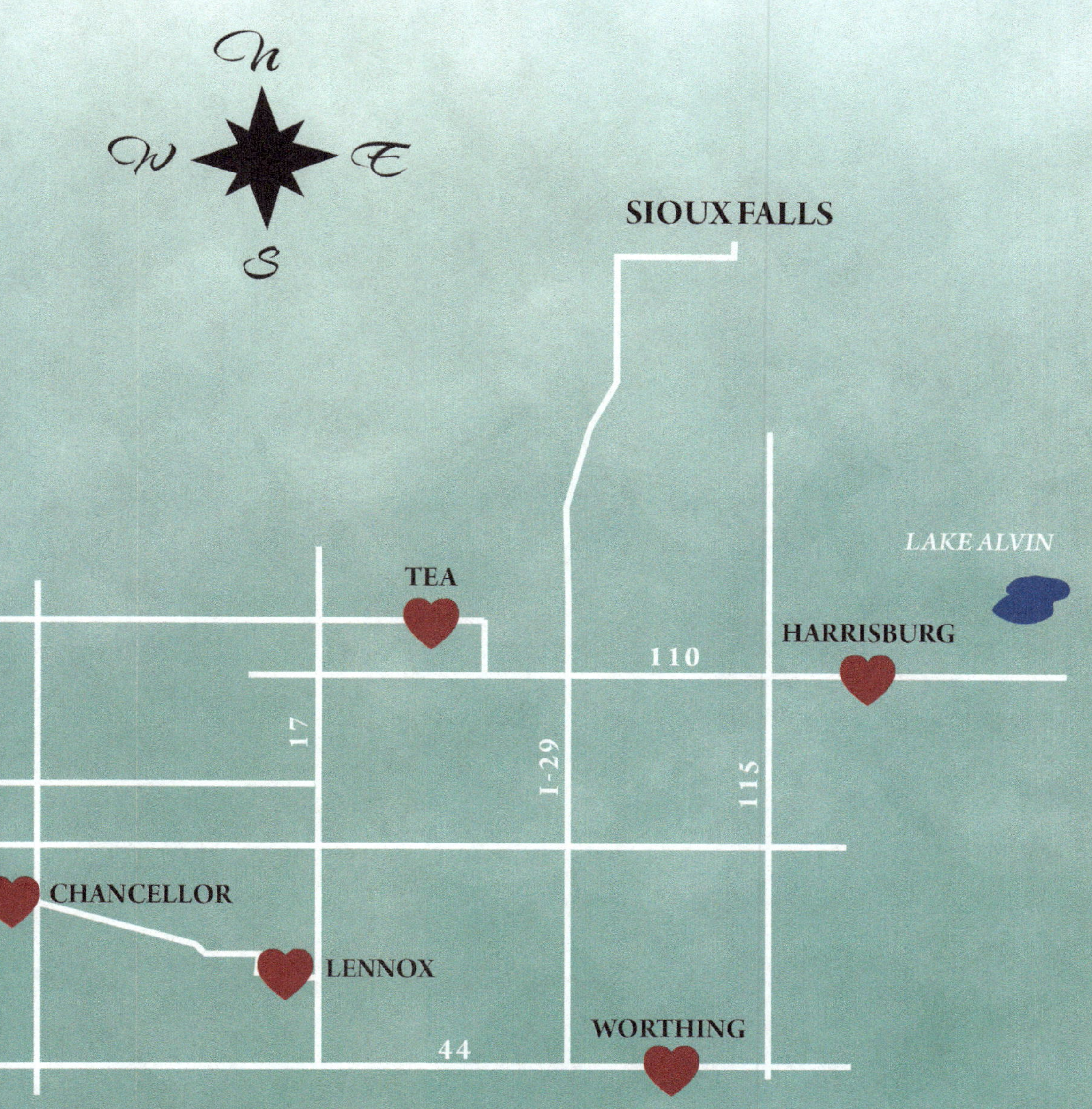

CHAPTER 8

HARVEST TRAIL

By now, we had traveled many miles and gathered a large array of photos. Selecting the winning photo for this chapter was a very hard decision. Or, I guess, maybe not. I just love pumpkins. The season of fall has always been my favorite time of year and each picture you see here filled with bright orange, yellow, greens, and browns depicts that.

My driver and I were as opposite in our thoughts, ideas, and likes as two people can be. His favorite season was spring. As you can imagine, it took some time for us to figure out how the other person in the vehicle was thinking and work through the details. I believe God must have a great sense of humor, locking us two bull-headed creatures together for months in a pickup. He is probably still chuckling over some of our never-to-be-told stories. Now in our fifth month, we were still alive and well, and we were having fun!

When the trumpet sounds here in the Midwest, harvest jumps into action, a bevy of excitement fills the air and busyness takes control. The gravel roads we routinely had to ourselves were now filled with tractors, combines, pickups, grain haulers, and families that were bringing parts, supplies, and food to the hard workers. Often with just a small window of opportunity to harvest the crop, many times the process would go well into the night and occasionally around the clock.

Driver and Miss Kelley reminisced driving their first tractors, the little A and B John Deere, and sharing all the stories that went along with those experiences. Comparing our first little tractors to the modern giants of today, we were now feeling a little disbelief at how quickly time had passed and how much things had changed. Crop-farming today seems to have the same basic principles we grew up with, but complexity, size, and speed are enormously different.

Whether or not we wanted the title, we were now the seniors of this world watching this exciting harvest through the windows of our pickup, just as the seniors during our youth did. We knew the season of harvest, the difficult and long hard days, the hopes, dreams, and many prayers said, but we also knew goodness and joy with each day's end. Our provisions were met and God's rich blessings of abundance brought nourishment to all in our country and around the world.

The winds of change were quietly filling the air, and we were assessing whether we could finish this journey before winter. We understood time was limited, having celebrated my early October birthday many times in a snowstorm. With a somewhat lengthy list of items yet to photograph and a few communities still waiting for our visit, this peaceful adventure was about to pick up speed.

Miss Kelley and Driver were holding in their hearts some little wishes neither had shared with the other. One of those wishes was about to come true on the day when we accidentally drove up to a church we had already photographed and, in total amazement, we both shouted, "Look at the windows!" The church was alive with a beauty we had not seen before, as each window reflected the most vivid colors imaginable. Throughout the entire building, light from the setting sun was illuminating every stained-glass window, and what a sight we were seeing! I recognized this brief God-given moment and quickly started snapping photos.

After sunset, we discussed this unique happening, suddenly realizing we both had secretly dreamed of a day when we would be blessed to discover a church with its windows glowing. This was the moment our wishes had been granted.

Produce was now ready for harvest and was found just about anywhere we traveled. Vendors were finding ways to sell their rich bounty, while dealing with the Covid virus, more or less creating their own set of rules when it came to handling the produce.

With masked proprietors on duty, some offered produce from under bright, colorful, eye-catching tents, while others set up little tables full of corn, potatoes, and onions with notes attached instructing us to simply drop our money in the box. Tomatoes, green beans, and cucumbers were also filling many pantries and the excess produce would often be found sitting along a curb with a note attached that read, "Free! Help yourself."

Animals seemed to stir up and bring frenzy into our quiet drives.

Any time an unsuspecting animal approached the road, my driver immediately began hitting the horn, racing the engine, and yelling loudly. The chase was on! For a brief moment, wild excitement filled our truck, and we were back in the good old days. Up until this moment, dogs, cats, and other animals were never seen. Or, perhaps they had been there all along, just wisely hiding.

Our long to-find list of evasive animals was trying its best to grab our attention and bring discouragement. We wondered how long the good weather would continue, and if we would successfully capture photos of all the animals on our lists, since most were quite lively and probably not as cooperative as a tree.

On this particular day, glancing into the driveway of a farm, something caught our eye, and we pulled in to grab a quick photo and be on our way. But soon we were finding more and more camera opportunities. To make a long story short, the farmer joined us and lovingly shared all his handmade creations, even leading us to his garage where he revealed his true work of art, a beautiful bright red classic hot-rod. My, what a beauty! We had a great visit, made a new friend and I finally had a photo of a cat and dog. I could happily scratch those two items off my list!

A few minutes later, a couple of miles down the road, I again glanced down a driveway and spotted pumpkins—my weakness—and quickly suggested we go in for a better look. This was the cornucopia of blessings and a wonderful place to visit! It was full of produce, pumpkins, squash, home-canned salsa, and other vegetables. But the real excitement of the day came when we spotted a menagerie of pets, each curiously watching as they mingled throughout the yard. There were chickens and ducks, cats, pigs, cows, and other animals too numerous to mention, each with a unique name letting everyone know they were special. We were encouraged to snap pictures to our heart's content, and that I did! Each animal was well aware of being a celebrity and loved "hamming it up" for the camera, and of course, this photographer loved taking their pictures!

We had been concerned about finishing our to-do list before the winter weather set in, thinking to ourselves, *it may be a long shot* for this to happen. But within a blink of an eye, whether we had little wishes or big prayers, "Someone" had lovingly met each of our needs. Yes, on this day, it was abundantly raining cats, dogs, and many other animals. Except for wild turkeys, our list was complete, and we gave thanks.

We were in the season of harvest now being led to each of our golden fields of memories. We knew we had been richly blessed with a "bumper crop," and we were leaving our footprints in the rich, black dirt and enjoying every moment that we knew we may never see again.

Meeting our goal was coming fast and all seemed to be going well. Unbeknownst to us we were about to begin one of the most uncomfortable, traumatic, and power-filled moments of our adventure. Wonder asked if we were prepared for what was about to come?

Don't forget to search for the big red heart hidden in plain sight in each of the following towns!

CHANCELLOR

Chancellor was established in 1886, named after Otto von Bismarck, Chancellor of the German Empire. This small town is home to the Poet Biorefining Plant, which utilizes over 35 million bushels of locally grown corn and processes it into 110 million gallons of ethanol annually. www.poet.com/chancellor

"POET Bioprocessing"-Chancellor, SD

LENNOX

Lennox, originally known as Ben Lennox, had its beginning in 1879 when the Milwaukee railroad came into town. Thursday evenings throughout the summer, Lennox offers the longest-running band concert in South Dakota. The city's rich history is lovingly preserved at the Lennox Museum. Be sure and stop in for a visit. www.cityoflennoxsd.com

WORTHING

Worthing was originally laid out in 1879 and named Worthington after a Milwaukee railroad conductor, but was later shortened to Worthing. Its motto has been, "A quiet place to call home." However, since 1990, its population has more than doubled, and Worthing now claims a new motto, "City of Pride, Progress & Possibilities."
www.cityofworthing.com

TEA

Tea was established in 1894 and is named after the tradition of drinking afternoon tea. Teapot Days, a community gathering filled with family fun, is celebrated each summer. The Tea Museum is filled with a beautiful collection of teapots, and is a definite must-see! The Marv Skie/Lincoln County Airport in Tea is the busiest in South Dakota.
www.teasd.com/history-of-tea

HARRISBURG

Harrisburg, a city in Lincoln County, now a suburb of Sioux Falls, moved its community several times before officially becoming a town in 1890. A legend surrounds this community: Tales are told of a daring bank robbery with bullet holes in the teller cabinet that remain as proof today.
www.harrisburgsd.gov

State Parks & Recreational Areas

LAKE ALVIN RECREATION AREA

GOOD EARTH STATE PARK

Harvest Trail Legacy Love Notes

On (date):___________ I found the hearts at: ________________

____

____

What I like the most was: ______________________________

____

Joy From the Trip

____

____

____

____

____

____

____

____

____

____

Lake Country Trail

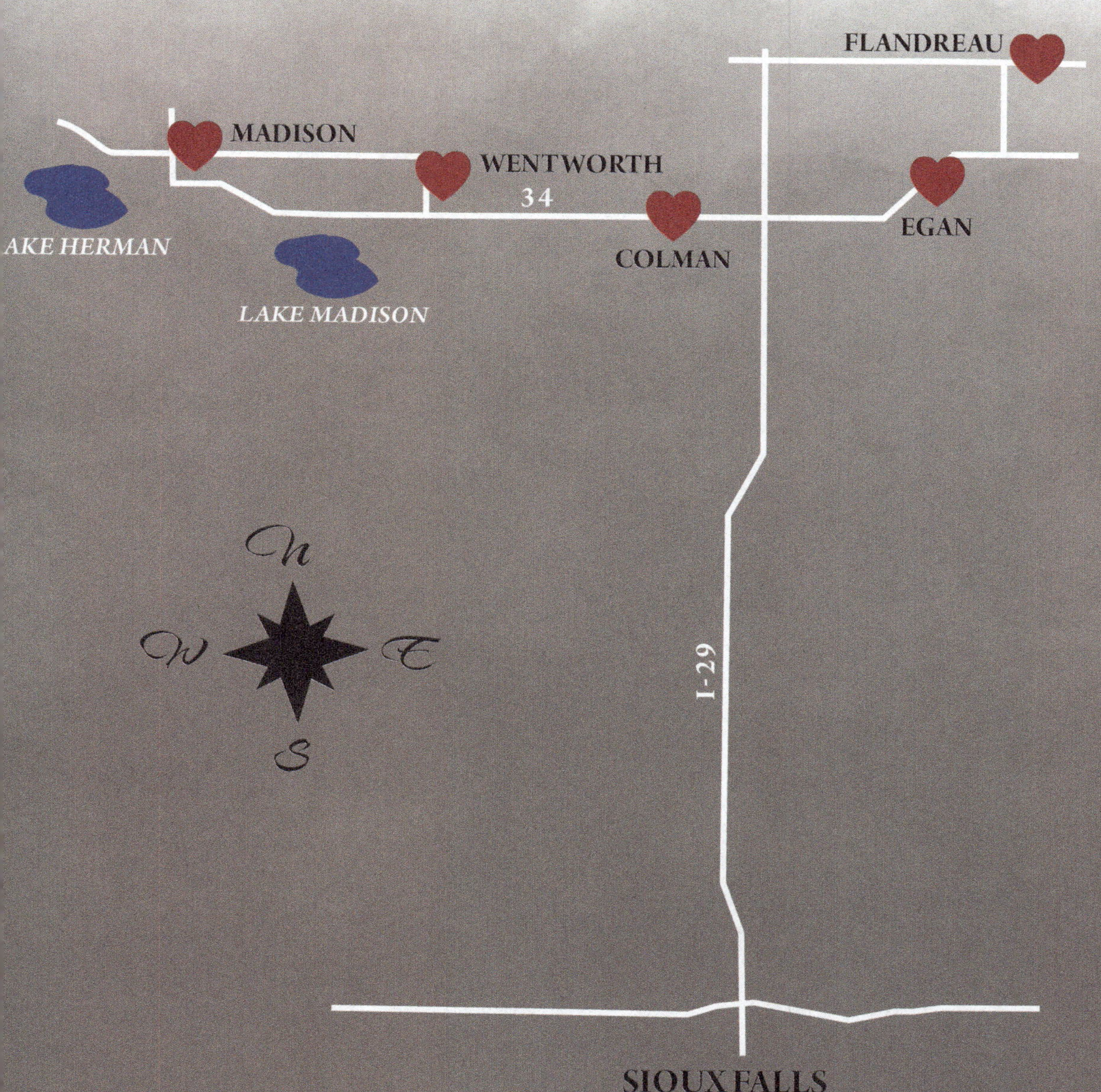

CHAPTER 9

LAKE COUNTRY TRAIL

With each sunrise comes a new day. As we stretch and wiggle our toes and prepare for each day, we wonder if it will be peaceful and calm, or full of surprises…and so it is with a lake.

Lakes can be the perfect atmosphere of enjoyment, ideal for fishing, boating, swimming, or watching a beautiful sunset. Have you ever planned what you thought to be a perfect day at the lake and found out otherwise? Each lake is influenced by bright blue skies, the warmth from the sun, gentle breezes, ominous storm clouds, strong winds, heavy rains, and many other forces that can instantly change a lake's disposition.

Driver and Miss Kelley were no strangers to lakes. We were now exploring that which, for most of my life, had been an extension of my backyard, having been born and raised a few short miles from this area called Lake Country. This trail felt like home to us, as it was one of our more familiar trails.

Both of us grew up with fishing poles in our hands and we had accumulated many fishing buckets full of stories. It was quite a conversation when we shared all of those wild and crazy moments. Of course, like most fishing stories, the tales told grew rapidly in size. We also experienced what every fisherman has probably already encountered, planning that perfect day at the lake, driving the distance, and upon arrival, being met with fierce, treacherous white caps and a lake totally out of control, warning everyone to stay clear and just leave it alone. Our reactions were always the same. In loud voices for all to hear, we would shout a well-used saying from our days of old, "Well, this is a fine kettle of fish!" We were there to *fish* and being turned away was not part of our plan.

The lake had its moments, and if you ignored its warnings, you might regret your decision. A special friend and I learned that the hard way back in the 1960s when we sank two rental boats in our first 24 hours on the lake. After a shore full of kind-hearted people braved the treacherous cold water and pulled the two of us and our three little puppies to safety, we quickly learned we were to respect these highly emotional bodies of water. On a good day, they were enjoyable, and on a bad day the lake was capable of bringing all types of destruction, occasionally taking lives, property, and stealing hope for the future.

The Covid-19 virus was still with us and its destruction was very evident with the U.S. reporting over 200,000 deaths by early September of 2020. Each day that toll continued to climb. Until now we had kept ourselves busy and focused on whatever would take our minds off this sad and very scary subject.

Now entering the month of October, something new was about to shift our focus and take center stage: the 2020 United States Presidential Election. For the last five months, we had exchanged sadness for beauty, uncertainty for strength, and most of the time, even if for just a few moments, we were able to turn off the world, along with all the Covid threats. Together, we found peace and serenity.

With the new struggle of the election gripping our nation (and what a struggle it was) we were finding it much harder to turn off the world. Serenity was being replaced by hundreds of flags, banners and signs. Patriotism and politics followed us everywhere, many times infiltrating our personal space, thoughts, and discussions. And of course, we didn't always agree.

Life is full of ups and downs. We were no strangers to surprises, and knew very well how quickly things can change, which reminds me of my favorite embroidery work with the words, "Life is fragile; handle with prayer." A wise thought to live by and one we took part in earnestly throughout this unique journey.

We were having what one might define as a normal day until we bravely headed the pickup in a new direction and began venturing out of the areas we had known so well. Already feeling a little uncomfortable, we noticed some interesting animals that reinforced those feelings. We were being curiously watched by a couple of llamas.

I love animals, but capturing them on camera is quite another story. Living on the farm for many years gave me some insight into animal behavior, actually leading me to write my last high school term paper on this subject. However, I knew nothing about llamas.

I understood that no matter how curious and charming animals may appear, there was always the unknown, and my best approach was to assume they were having a "bad hair day" and keep my distance. Some are curious and others shy. If you watch closely, you may even notice that some can be sneaky. This, I noted the afternoon we learned a bit more about llamas while grabbing a few photos. *How hard could this be*?

They seemed friendly and curious enough to come right to the fence, making for a perfect shot with my little camera, except every time I tried to get close, my driver kept yelling, "Be careful! They spit!"

We played hide-and-seek for quite some time. As my camera went up, one llama teasingly hid behind the post, keeping one eye on me at all times, and when my camera came down, out popped his face. Through all my laughter, defensive dancing, and loud shouts from the pickup, I eventually snapped a couple of pictures. Are they winning photos? Probably not, but I guess you could say I was the real winner in this battle, for I knew a little more about llamas than when I started. And I was not covered in spit!

My driver told me later, if I had gotten any spit on me, he would not have welcomed me back into the truck. I am not sure just how that would have turned out.

We continued down this unknown path, finding beautiful rolling hills and autumn-colored valleys, with laughter and thoughts of llamas still keeping us company. Suddenly, everything changed. I had noticed a pumpkin display, and you know my weakness for pumpkins. *I needed a picture.*

We weren't close enough for what I thought to be a good shot. My normal routine would have been to open my door, jump out, take a few steps and snap the picture safely. For some reason, I was feeling uncomfortable. Something was not right, and for that moment, I felt compelled to stay in the pickup. Still questioning why I was feeling this way, I hesitantly opened the window to grab my quick shot.

At that very moment, a fast-moving pickup turned into this driveway. Instead of slowing down and calmly passing on the driver's side, with no hesitation he wildly drove between our pickup and the pumpkin display, missing my side of the truck by inches. In disbelief and total shock, Miss Kelley and Driver were both seeing the same vision, my lifeless body lying in twisted wreckage.

It was a very quiet road from that moment on as we silently gave thanks and continued to digest this shocking reminder of how vulnerable we are and how quickly our lives can change for better or worse.

Still very much shaken and emotional wounds wide open, within two miles, we found ourselves led to a beautiful country church. Standing reverently by its side were two unique steel cut-outs, the work of a local artist titled, "The Way" and "Victory over Death."

The sky, a soft blue just a few minutes earlier, now reflected the powerful beauty of this miraculous moment. I was safe and secure. I pondered all these things as I snapped each photo and climbed back into the pickup. With no words spoken, the floodgates opened and tears of thankfulness and joy overflowed.

When we find our happy place and settle in, we stop doing, seeing, and trying and become as stagnant as the waters in a polluted lake. A true lake basin needs a small stream of fresh water to keep the lake alive and clean. Without that fresh water, the lake will eventually die.

We, too, need to keep our lives fresh and healthy. Don't wait for the right moment or a special day. Now is the time to adjust our pathway in life, seek joy, carry a basket of goodness to others, and live each day to its fullest. Oh, how quickly everything can change and be gone!

We were ready for our last trail. Our memories were now taking center stage and preparing to reveal the greater picture. With most of our footprints in the past, we were about to explore the final trail and claim our victory. What were we about to discover?

"Thy Way"

"Victory Over Death"

"THE WAY" AND "VICTORY OVER DEATH"

"The Way" was sculpted by Allan C. Fisher and installed in 2006 at St. Peter Lutheran Church (now St. Peter of the Prairie). The sculpture is strategically placed on the outskirts of Madison, South Dakota, where there are no billboards or distracting buildings and is based on Biblical scripture – John 14:6 ("I am the way the truth and the life") and Psalm 23 ("I am the good shepherd").

Christ is holding the lamb affectionately like a Madonna and child. As a viewer, you can literally walk through the cutout body of Christ on a stone pathway. Allan said, "I am merely framing God's beauty." The sculpture is oriented east and west, so you can see the sunrise and sunset through the cutout. Because of the changing seasons, the changing atmospheres, the changing light, the sculpture is always changing.

"Victory Over Death" was sculpted by Allan C. Fisher and installed on July 24, 2008. Scripture is the inspiration for the sculpture perfectly situated on the outskirts of Madison, South Dakota, next to St. Peter Lutheran Cemetery. As the psalmist says, "The heavens declare the glory of God". Again, the sculpture frames God's beauty. The sky illuminates and brings the work alive. Designed as a monumental icon, it enables the viewer to reflect on the resurrection and the concept of breaking the barriers, light over darkness, joy over sorrow, hope over fear, and life over death. The work is a celebration, a triumph, representing the ultimate victory: Christ's victory over death.

Allan C. Fisher
Visual Artist/Owner
www.allancfisher.com
1-605-271-7115

Don't forget to search for the big red heart hidden in plain sight in each of the following towns!

EGAN

Egan was established when the Chicago, Milwaukee, and St. Paul railroad arrived in 1880. Today, it proudly claims the motto, "A small town with big hearts." Egan is the perfect place to raise a family and welcomes your visit.
www.egansd.com

2

1

FLANDREAU

Flandreau, since its founding, has been located in various places, had different spelling and name changes, and is one of the oldest cities in South Dakota. It is a small but progressive community, which claims the motto, "The Heart of Eastern South Dakota." For those seeking history, the City of Flandreau website offers great information on the Moody County Pioneers and Historic Sites around the area. www.cityofflandreau.com

2

1

3

COLMAN

Colman was originally named Allentown until 1890, when the railroad arrived and brought with it a new name for the community, Colman. This busy little city celebrates Looney Days each year in August. Come, join the fun!
www.colmansd.com

WENTWORTH

Wentworth, the only incorporated village in South Dakota, was platted in 1881 and named after the local Wentworth family. It is just a few miles from the Lakes Golf Course. Be sure and check it out!
www.wentworthsd.com

MADISON

Madison, in 1870, had its early beginnings on the southern shores of Lake Madison. Because of the railroad and an invitation to the residents of Madison from C.B. Kennedy in 1881 the community moved north to its present location. True to its motto, "Discover the unexpected," Madison celebrates South Dakota's only bacon festival, the Bacon Bash, every September.
www.cityofmadisonsd.com

State Parks & Recreational Areas

LAKE MADISON

LAKE HERMAN STATE PARK

LUCE FAMILY CEMETERY
JOHN ABBOT - MARY LUCE'S BROTHER. DIED WHEN LOST IN A BLIZZARD.
MARY ABBOT LUCE - THE SECOND WIFE OF HERMAN LUCE. DIED FROM INJURIES IN ACCIDENTAL FIRE.
MARY HOLMES ABBOT - MARY ABBOT LUCE'S MOTHER. DIED OF NATURAL CAUSE.
MARY LUCE - DAUGHTER OF MARY AND HERMAN LUCE. DIED OF CHICKEN POX.

FLANDREAU CITY PARK

WALKER'S POINT STATE RECREATION AREA

Lake Country Trail
Legacy Love Notes

On (date):____________ I found the hearts at: __________________

____

____

What I like the most was: _____________________________________

____

Joy From the Trip

____

____

____

____

____

____

____

____

____

____

Siouxland Trail

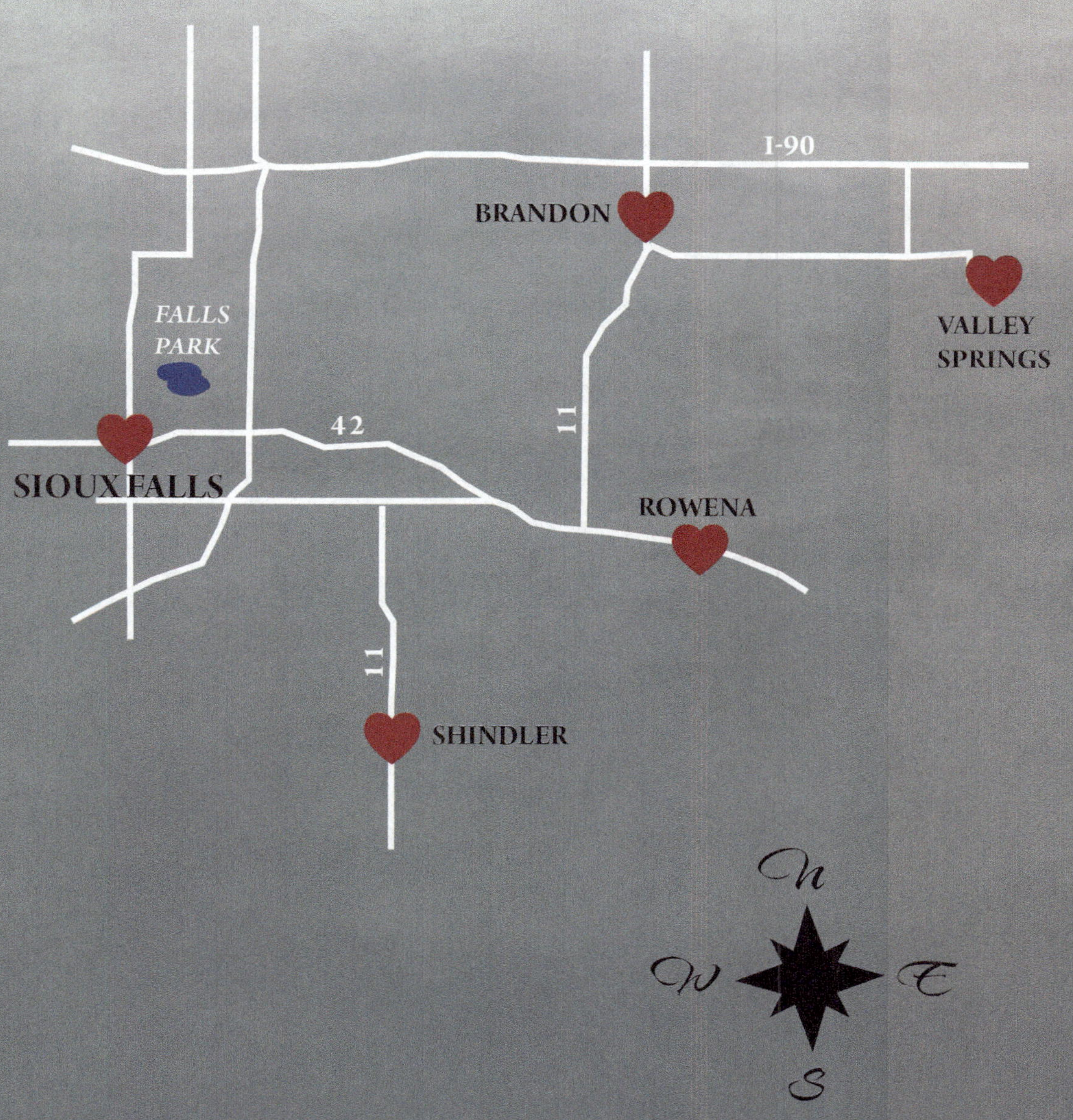

CHAPTER 10

SIOUXLAND TRAIL

Sandwiched in the middle of the 20th century Driver and Miss Kelley lived both old and new days, having had grandparents and parents who were early immigrants to America. In our youth we lived and touched the communities that our families helped build. We attended small one-room schools that stood alone in the middle of many farmers' fields, with its outhouse too far away to bother with on a cold winter's day.

We were young, but with the gift of memory, today we remember the steam-powered threshing machines and the frenzy of setting up all the oat-shocks before the crew arrived for harvest. The work and our chores were always there. We were being raised in the world of farming, and hard work was our teacher. Only those to whom the farm had been promised, or given a chance to buy or rent, would carry on.

As the doors closed behind us on that graduation evening, we were given notice it was time to try something different. The world was waiting. I am sure many of us had the same thoughts; we loved the farm. It had become our life, and that was all we knew. Struggling to answer the gnawing question, "Where do I go and what do I do?" we scattered like a flock of young chickens, searching for grain in the prairie grass, leaving behind what we had all come to know so well… home.

Today the Siouxland Trail is our home. It is no different from all the other trails. It may embody one much larger city than all the others. However, it still holds tightly to its original small-town charm, a big brother of sorts, sharing goodness and opportunity with its many neighbors.

Sioux Falls is a great place to start or finish; it has been the gathering place of many since its early beginnings, offering water and opportunity, a common thread found throughout the region. It filled the people's needs, and life was awakened, but its location was its strength. The real eye-opener that captured the attention of all, including many influential early settlers who now propelled the city into the future.

Living within the boundaries of Sioux Falls, you do not need to drive far to enjoy this well-kept land of the Sioux. Within just a few minutes, one can find themselves transported back into natural grasslands and trails of old that have been lovingly preserved for all.

When we began leaving the farm, the bigger cities called our names, and we accepted their offer for a new and exciting life. It was not one-stop shopping in the 1960s as we know it today. Higher places of learning were tucked in and around each community, large or small, college or otherwise, and all you needed to know was how to find them.

I made my choice: I would be a nurse. The program offered was considered an extension of the local high school, and the class setting was located in the basement of one of the local elementary schools.

Old and new crossed paths numerous times, in my early nursing days. Some of the "good old family doctors" continued to carry the old, black, tired, worn medical bags to each house call. In contrast, a new generation of doctors began to see a new vision.

The new healthcare system had come, and it was here to stay. After years and years of bedside pampering, the public had become spoiled, and they were now being asked to give up the luxury of house calls. It was a heart-wrenching decision for my doctor, one I watched him struggle with for years.

The early 20th century was slowly disappearing, and the second half of the century was busy guiding us toward the future. Urban sprawl continued eating away at our rural communities. Today, tired and worn remnants of the past continue to dot the horizon, but with a keen eye, you may spot many more in hiding, still waiting to be found. Our small country schools are no more. School buildings were sold, demolished, or bought by local farmers to be used as extra buildings for their animals. The rural farm kids boarded the big yellow buses and headed into town. Our favorite outhouses were set on fire and we began buying real toilet paper—no more peach wrappers or old magazines!

Not to change the subject, but it had been almost nine months since Covid first came on the scene, bringing the worldwide toilet paper shortage with it. I believe everyone now has a much greater appreciation for the soft, gentle kindness of that roll of paper.

We were soon to cross the finish line and our thoughts were swirling everywhere. We had been enjoying secluded picnics, hot dog roasts, and hiding in our pickup full of snacks for nearly nine months. According to my calculations, we had probably consumed enough goodies to fill a barn, so what does that say about our waistlines and poor abused teeth? I wondered when life began again and our missed appointments were rescheduled, would our dentists, doctors, or anybody for that fact, even recognize us?

With just a few towns yet to visit, Miss Kelley and Driver were about to accomplish their goal. We had searched every large to practically non-existent town, community, lake, and park within a fifty-mile radius of Sioux Falls, and captured every photo on our list, except turkeys.

I noticed sadness slowly creeping into my thoughts, as wonder began teasing repeatedly with, *Now what?* This entire journey had brought us the gift of love, treasured photos, and memories that would never be forgotten. Hating to say goodbye, I was beginning to feel the loss. This was going to be tough. My driver, who, most of the time at all costs, kept his emotions hidden, quietly continued his drive. Unknown to me, he was also sensing change.

After our last official trip, my driver suggested we return to the same area the next day, as he wanted to pick up something. I didn't question a repeat. How could I say no to another exciting day?

A short time later, we found ourselves again on a gravel road. After Driver made his purchase, I was given a quick hug and handed a cute metal scarecrow. He knew how much Miss Kelley loved fall, and this was for her! The camera was now focused on the two of us for the first time. We had come to the end of the trail, and this was our moment to celebrate!

After listening to our brief story and snapping the final picture, our new "trail angel" and sweet farm gal said her goodbyes. We were finished and could have headed home, but instead, we climbed back into the pickup and continued exploring, neither of us ready to quit.

Four thousand miles was a lengthy drive, but somehow it felt short. It had given us hours to reflect and think. We dug around in our memories, thinking about the freedoms of adulthood, of love, and the chaos of family life, the pain of the empty nest, and eventually, the end of our earthly trail.

We spoke of our thoughts often and found we were both feeling a much deeper sense of love, gratitude, and respect for all who had come before us and made America what it is today. Now in our season of harvest, we questioned our fruits of love and how those remnants would affect the next generation. We recognized the importance of the past, for without it, there would be no present or future.

The twentieth century had gone by in the blink of an eye. I remember the photos of my stern-looking grandparents, wondering if they ever smiled. I recalled the spankings I received for my misbehavior, the quick reprimands I was given when a bad word was spoken, and the consequences for all wrongs committed. I thought about the love for one another and caring, kind neighbors who became our forever friends.

We loved this country and took pride in our communities. I remember taking pride in working hard, being a part of this great country, and dressing in our finest clothes every Sunday when we entered the Lord's house. We shared many meals, enjoyed our elders, and listened intently to their stories, for they had a wealth of goodness to pass on. As most of us do, we had our moments, but we still loved and respected our parents, said our prayers, and learned forgiveness.

As today's world seems to spin out of control, we must remember the goodness and wonder of the past that has made us who we are. Each moment is a gift, and each memory holds the key to our future.

We have crossed the finish line. This journey has been the adventure of our lifetime. Together, Driver and Miss Kelley forged the prairies and explored every inch of the Ten Trails of the Heartland, discussing everything from "soup to nuts" and unearthing wagon loads of history and memories that had been buried for years.

For the last six months, we watched intently through the windows of the truck and searched deeply into each community. Not only did we gain greater insight, knowledge, and enjoyment from this journey, but we had also become a part of the picture. It was evident our lives would never be the same.

Don't forget to search for the big red heart hidden in plain sight in each of the following towns!

VALLEY SPRINGS

Valley Springs was named after the springs of the nearby Beaver Creek Valley. It lies close to the South Dakota and Minnesota border and claims the title, "Front Door to South Dakota."
www.cityofvalleysprings.com

BRANDON

Brandon was established by the railroad and platted in 1878, although homesteaders (mostly of Scandinavian and German descent) had been here for a decade prior. In 1950, there were only 250 residents, but today there are more than 10,000 citizens. Recently Brandon has been in the news thanks to native Dale Moss, who starred in the 2020 season of the reality television show *The Bachelorette*.
www.cityofbrandon.org

3

4

ROWENA

Rowena was built on an abundance of red jasper and granite. It was platted and founded in 1888 by the Illinois Central railroad and today remains an unincorporated community. Two of South Dakota's tallest structures, the KELO and KDLT television towers, are located near Rowena and have a history of their own to tell.

1

2

SHINDLER

Shindler was known by a few different names until 1891 when it officially reclaimed its original name. In 1910, a new town hall was completed which soon became the social hub of the city where dances, Sunday school and school functions were held. In the 1930s, failed crops and drought created problems that would eventually shut down the post office in 1953 and end what had been known as the town of Shindler.

SIOUX FALLS

Sioux Falls was founded in 1857 by land speculators and named for the Sioux Tribe of American Indians and the waterfalls of the Big Sioux River. It is considered one of the healthiest cities in the United States to live in, according to Best Life magazine. A gathering place for many, it has grown to become the largest city in the state of South Dakota. Filled with abundant blessings, Sioux Falls has more than 70 parks and greenways. With all the amenities of a large city, Sioux Falls continues to hold tight to its friendly small-town charm. Recently, Sioux Falls was named the #5 best place to live in America by livability.com.
www.experiencesiouxfalls.com

"Sioux Falls Reflecting in a Woman's Glasses."
by mural artist Jillian Gunlicks, Brandon SD

State Parks & Recreational Areas

ARROWHEAD PARK SIOUX FALLS

BIG SIOUX STATE RECREATION AREA

GREAT BEAR RECREATION PARK
SIOUX FALLS

"Bear Lee Standing" sculpture artist Gary Hovey, Ohio. Winner of the 15th annual Sioux Falls SculptureWalk People's Choice award.

BEAVER CREEK STATE NATURE AREA

FALLS PARK, SIOUX FALLS

Siouxland Trail Legacy Love Notes

On (date):__________ I found the hearts at: ______________

____

____

What I like the most was: ______________________

____

Joy From the Trip

____

____

____

____

____

____

____

____

____

____

CONCLUSION

SUNSET TRAIL

Moment by moment, day by day, our travels had led us deeper into the heart of rural America. The year 2020 was a very sad and difficult time for our world and our country, but with each small wonder and unique treasure discovered, Miss Kelley and Driver were experiencing happiness and their smiles were filling the air. We found our "senior moments" the most entertaining. But, as they say, "Laughter is the best medicine," and those moments were healing to our soul.

When we first started this journey we were simply looking for a perfect picture, one that would win a contest. But soon we realized this journey was not about one unique picture. In reality, we were seeking joy and happiness. Surrounded by uncertainty, anxiety and loss we were led to quiet pastures, peaceful meadows, and bountiful harvests.

We were drawn to each church. I loved the beauty of the soft blue sky and each steeple proudly holding the cross high enough to be seen for miles. For a brief moment, I was there, hearing "Lift High the Cross" and "Praise God from Whom all Blessings Flow." I could only imagine the joyous sound of all the church bells ringing throughout the valleys and countryside every Sunday morning.

After traveling six months, driving around 4,000 miles, and intensely exploring every nook and cranny of the vast Heartland region, we noticed something different. With our eyes wide open, we better understood each community, the people, and their history. Passion, gratitude, love for one another and those around us that we had not known before filled out hearts. Each community became our home as we gathered memories. We were two old people, returning to our youth, as patrol watching over the crops, quiet strangers praying for those in need. With each footstep, we had become a part of each community.

During the early days of our journey, we found what we thought to be joy but soon realized it was only superficial. Just a fleeting moment, it was a distraction to keep us from looking further. We were seeking joy that could not be extinguished; joy that would satisfy and bring peace; joy that would strengthen and help us through our most difficult moments. We needed joy that would protect and direct us along each path, bringing forgiveness, freedom, and love to all.

Deep in the heart of pain and sorrow, like a seed planted in rich, black dirt, we grew, and the harvest was the fullness of joy!

Psalm 16: 11 tells, "You will make known to me the path of life; In Your presence is fullness of joy; In Your right hand there are pleasures forever." (NASB 1995)

We assessed our trip. Everything we had hoped to find, including most animals and birds, had now been officially captured in a photo, except for the elusive turkey. In truth, I didn't push the issue, as any feathery creature was not something I would get too close to and for sure not chase around! Wild turkeys are rarely seen in the bigger cities, so we had quite a surprise a couple of weeks later when a flock of turkeys decided to come and find us! Patiently strolling in the backyard, even posing nicely on the deck rail, they were ready for their picture, and my list was complete!

After officially leaving our footprints in every community, lake, and park within the Ten Trails of the Heartland, driving many more country roads than planned, and snapping photos beyond reason, the hunt was over.

"As for us, our life is like grass. We grow and flourish like a wild-flower, then the wind blows on it, and it is gone-no one sees it again." Psalm 103:15-16 (GNT)

Today "we the people" stand bravely on the prairie within a raging pandemic. Just as our forefathers experienced pain and sorrow, they found faith to carry them through. With each setback, they found the strength to start anew. As the sun sets each day and the night fills with darkness, we rest upon the Lord and wait for the return of the sun! We begin again.

"Would you like to go for a ride, Miss Kelley?" These words ignite a blaze of memories, never to be forgotten.

Wherever your journey takes you, choose to include my friend Jesus. He has already experienced this same trail. He knows all the pitfalls and has given His life that we may find everlasting life in His presence. He will take your boring, confused, painful, messed-up life and put you back on the right path.

You may be wondering, "What do I need to do?" Simply say this prayer, "Jesus, I am sorry for all the wrongs I have done. Please forgive me and come into my heart." At that moment Jesus will be your guide forever. The Bible is your handbook! It is power-packed with joy and love for each step of your journey! Follow it diligently.

TRAILBLAZER HANDBOOK

- This is the day to seek joy. Prayer will give you direction.
- You have a guide that loves you; He will lead the way.
- Pay attention, expect the unexpected, and remember that corrections may be needed.
- Distractions and struggles will block the way. Be persistent and never give up.
- There will be many trails to choose from, but the good of others will always be the right path.
- When you need help, pray. Your guide is listening.
- To have freedom in your journey, remember where you started.
- Should you need anything, it will be provided.
- Be prepared and stay nourished; things can change quickly.
- Before the trail ends, leave a few footprints and share your journey so that others may also find joy.
- And never forget to say, "Thank you!"

NOTE OF APPRECIATION

When we hold joy in our hands, it warms the heart.
When we share where we have been, it lights the way.

I am so thankful for all who caught my vision and accepted my challenge to be "Keeper of the Heart." I liked the idea of inviting others to seek the heart of each town. I didn't realize what an incredible mountain I was yet to climb to achieve my dream, or the blessings that would follow.

These bright and beautiful red hearts may tell the story of where I have been and the joy I have found, but when displayed proudly within each town, they will be a reflection of the love shared between neighbors and friends and the goodness each community brings to others. Together, all 51 hearts will bring light to the world.

The following are some of the encouraging notes sent to me during this season of worldwide pandemic in response to some efforts I've made to bring smiles with my drawings and cards with notes to help lighten the load.

It is my honor and privilege to introduce you to just a few of my many friends and pioneers who have lovingly preserved and now pass this beautiful land we call home to a new generation.

"Dear Lonnette, I'm not at all sure how to begin this note to someone so positive and encouraging to me. I enjoy my little animal cards. I looked forward to receiving them and am re-reading and looking at them every day. The painting is beautiful. I have shown them to my friends but can't part with them. I am a retired teacher and at my age started teaching in country schools. I have seen a lot of changes but the worst is this Covid-19, which seems to be unstoppable right now. Stay safe! Thank you!"

— *Orpha*

"Thanks for the series of hope. I enjoyed it and have most of the pictures. I am 100 years old and just can't take any more writing so this will be short. Thank you and God bless you."

— *Edna*

"Special thoughts of you—Lonnette, thank you for the little animal smiles. That is a very wonderful thing you are doing. I have lived on a farm in the area for 80 years and have been married for 61 years. With the uncertainty in today's world, I still have lots to be thankful for. People like you make the world a better place!"

— *Joyce*

"Dear Lonnette, Thank you for the Christmas greetings. It was nice to receive your card since most people are not sending them this year… it is hard for me to get into the Christmas Spirit anyway since it was this time of year my husband died, and our anniversary was always celebrated. This year has been especially hard with the virus doing so much damage to friends and relatives since no family gatherings can be planned. You have done your part in trying to bring joy to people. Thank you for being so thoughtful. Have a blessed holiday season, and do stay healthy."

— *Bonnie, age 96*

Blessings surround us every day, and they often come in pairs. We give, we receive, joy fills our hearts, and love grows.

If you are planning to experience this trip, I would truly enjoy hearing of the treasures discovered, lessons learned and the impact it made on your life.

Please send all notes to www.lonnettekelley.com

Lonnette Kelley is also available for speaking engagements and seminars. Please contact her at lonnettekelley556@gmail.com

ACKNOWLEDGMENTS

We are all on this journey called life. From one day to the next, we venture life's many pathways toward the finish line on earth that we call death. We never know what each day may hold. Unexpected turns in the road, hills that block our view, or obstacles that get in our way, lead us to peaceful meadows that refresh our souls and bring strength to continue our journey.

First and foremost, I say thank you and give all the glory of this amazing journey to my Lord and Savior Christ Jesus! Without His amazing grace, love, and guidance, I would still be lost somewhere along life's way.

Philippians 3:14 says, "I press on to reach the end of the race and receive the heavenly prize for which God, through Christ Jesus, is calling us."

Thank you to my trusty fun-loving driver for being my chauffeur over all these miles. The many moments you held your breath and said quiet prayers as you watched me be...well, me! We were quite a team! This wild and crazy adventure would never have been the same without you.

Thank you, Jeremy Brown and the Throne Publishing team. You captured my vision. Filled with Godly inspiration, you brought life and energy to my journey, creating a beautiful legacy of adventure for others to experience and enjoy.

Thank you, dear friends, for your many acts of kindness and generosity. A book requires an army of beautiful people to succeed. You are special. You make this world a better place, and you have helped make this book a reality!

And not to be forgotten, thank you to my beautiful family for loving me, encouraging me, and sharing your goodness. You inspire me and fill my heart with memories and joy that will last my lifetime!

ABOUT THE AUTHOR

Lonnette Kelley is no stranger to farm life. Growing up in southwestern Minnesota, she helped work the black fields and abundant harvests. Lonnette served most of her 55 years as a nurse in South Dakota with brief assignments in Nebraska and North Dakota. Her creative and entrepreneurial spirit has continuously tugged for attention throughout her life. Besides her nursing career, she also ran a bed and breakfast, where her most celebrated honor came in 1999 when the President of Iceland chose to stay at her establishment at 221 Melsted Place in Mountain, North Dakota.

Then during the worldwide Covid-19 pandemic, Lonnette had another "tug" on her heart to create "The Eyes of God" ministry: simple hand-painted cards featuring wide-eyed animals that could break the barriers of isolation by bringing smiles and love to those suffering loneliness and despair. To date, she has placed over 4,000 cards of hope into the hands of those in need.

To find healing and peace for herself in the middle of all the sadness, Lonnette enjoyed beautiful drives through nature which eventually led her to explore over 4,000 miles of what she calls God's Country, the Heartland of southeastern South Dakota.

Knowing the love of the Lord, Lonnette is inspired to reach out to others and share her walk of faith through her writings, photography, speaking, and encouraging thoughts, that others may also find joy in the presence of God.

Blessed with a son and daughter, four grandchildren, two great-grandchildren, two sisters, and their families, Lonnette's passion is hospitality. She can be found cooking and gathering family and friends around her dining table where she lovingly spoils and gives thanks for each moment they can be together. Lonnette understands how quickly life can change after losing her son.

Visit www.lonnettekelley.com to keep up with Lonnette and all her adventures.

Made in the USA
Monee, IL
20 May 2023

33560855R00129